STEAM IN THE EAST MIDLANDS & LINCOLNSHIRE

A PICTORIAL JOURNEY IN THE LATE 1950s AND EARLY 1960s

STEAM IN THE EAST MIDLANDS & LINCOLNSHIRE

A PICTORIAL JOURNEY IN THE LATE 1950s AND EARLY 1960s

RODERICK H FOWKES

PEN & SWORD
TRANSPORT

First published in Great Britain in 2018 by
Pen and Sword Transport

An imprint of Pen & Sword Books Limited
47 Church Street , Barnsley, South Yorkshire
S70 2AS

ISBN: 978 1 47389 629 1

Typeset by Aura Technology and Software Services, India
Printed and bound in India by Replika Press Pvt. Ltd

Pen & Sword Books Limited incorporates the imprints of Atlas, Archaeology, Aviation, Discovery, Family History, Fiction, History, Maritime, Military, Military Classics, Politics, Select, Transport, True Crime, Air World, Frontline Publishing, Leo Cooper, Remember When, Seaforth Publishing, The Praetorian Press, Wharncliffe Local History, Wharncliffe Transport, Wharncliffe True Crime and White Owl.

For a complete list of Pen & Sword titles please contact
PEN & SWORD BOOKS LIMITED
47 Church Street, Barnsley, South Yorkshire, S70 2AS, United Kingdom
E-mail: enquiries@pen-and-sword.co.uk
Website: www.pen-and-sword.co.uk

CONTENTS

ACKNOWLEDGEMENTS

I am greatly indebted to Martyn Reeve for allowing me access to photographs from the many albums of the late M.E.Kirk collection. Also, special thanks to Tony Smith and Joe Wade for their unstinting patience whilst sifting through their photographic collections; Michael Draper, for his assistance on railway matters;

Tim Hudson for permission to use the General Map of Rail Connections with Lincoln and last, but not least, Paul Harvey of Icarus Media and James Garratt at Milepost 92½ who diligently scanned the pictures and to John Scott-Morgan the commissioning editor for Pen & Sword, who kindly sanctioned the book.

FOREWORD

Many of the photographs in this book were taken by the late M. E. Kirk, who by profession was a schoolteacher; he undertook many forays not only in England but also Ireland and on the continent during his teaching tenure photographing predominantly steam with some diesel locomotives, also trams and trolley buses. His vast collection, most of which are captioned on the actual photograph or in the many albums, were rescued for posterity by Martyn Reeve. Whilst avoiding a detailed history of the present stations that are still in use, where more detailed accounts are available elsewhere, the focus on routes and stations long since closed, and were not all as a result of the Beeching report.

From the austere days of the early Nationalisation era, images of both locomotives and rolling stock were continually changing. During the transitional period, a few locomotives from the Big Four were turned out in various shades of green and blue, no doubt to gauge the public reaction alongside the coaching stock. Also in evidence was the lettering BRITISH RAILWAYS in full on the tender, which would remain until the adoption of the 'Lion and Wheel' totem in 1949. Often referred to as the 'ferret and dartboard' this was replaced in 1956 by 'a demi-lion rampant with a silver locomotive wheel held between the paws emerging from a heraldic crown complete with insignias of Great Britain', with a British Railways legend. The emblem was also displayed on coaching stock. Never having seen an '8P' (Coronation/Gresley A4) engine in blue livery, these handsome and extremely powerful locomotives were soon to be adorned in B.R. Brunswick Green, already applied to other locos in the higher power ranges. In 1957, however, the LMR adopted a maroon colour for their ex-LMS Pacifics, thereby transforming those great engines.

Coaching stock values also changed with some embellished in experimental liveries. The 'Plum and Spilt Milk' colour of the Main-line corridor coaches gave way to 'Crimson Lake and Cream', also referred to as 'Blood and Custard'. Restored to a limited extent in 1954 by the then British Transport Commission, who decreed that Corporate Liveries – Chocolate and Cream for the Western, Green for the Southern – within limitations be reintroduced, which in 1957 became the norm. Gradually (SR excepted) Maroon livery was to be the uniform colour throughout until the mid-1960s when Blue with Grey upper panels would become standard.

In 1957, the London Midland Region again ran weekly excursion 'holiday expresses' from Birmingham, Coventry, Northampton, Wolverhampton, Luton, Derby, Nottingham, Mansfield and Leicester. A special non-stop cafeteria express, with a guaranteed seat, ran to a different resort on five days of the week. The trains left after breakfast and returned in the late evening. Inclusive fares for the week ranged from 50 shillings. An example of the 1950s holiday express was one from Leicester during the city's holiday weeks. It went to North Wales on Monday, Southend on Tuesday, Skegness on Wednesday, London on Thursday, and Blackpool on Friday.

INTRODUCTION

We start our journey through the East Midlands beginning at Derby with a look at the various motive power in the station from the 1950s and a brief visit around the shed and works. The station, opened in 1839, was renamed Derby Midland in September 1950 and two years later extensive rebuilding took place at a cost of £200,000 using pre-stressed concrete and involving the complete demolition of the Stephenson train shed, the work being completed in 1954.

The annual horticultural show incorporating the Derby Locomotive Works Open Day always produced massive crowds. The star attraction was usually a locomotive not normally seen in the Derby area, that ranged from a 'Royal Scot' or a 'Britannia' in the early 1950s to the ultimate, a member of the 'Coronation' class, the likes of the appropriately named *City of Nottingham* No. 46251 or 46256 *Sir William Stanier F.R.S.* The neighbouring motive power depot was out of bounds to the visitors, cordoned off and patrolled by BTC police; despite this, though, there were quite a number of spotters who found an alternative way in.

Steam engines awaiting a berth in the Locomotive Works conglomerated in sidings adjacent to Deadmans Lane. In April 1951, the new BR Standard Class '5' 4-6-0 No. 73000 appeared from the shops; these and other of the larger engines released ex-works often had a trial run to Trent and back. When arriving at Derby station by train from the south, it was nigh impossible to see the numbers of locos on shed that stood behind the front line. During the morning, a raft of ex-works locomotives would be hauled out of one of the outside shed roads towards Engine Shed Sidings signal box before being propelled back again, their motions

making a hissing noise although devoid of steam. Nevertheless, these were engines whose numbers had up to that point been unobtainable.

In the early 1950s, to the delight of train spotters, there was an Anglo-Scottish transfer of half-a-dozen long serving 'Jubilees' between the Midland Division and depots at Kingmoor (Carlisle), Perth and Glasgow. Other unusual visitors were locomotives for overhaul at Derby Locomotive Works; which would include those from East London (Plaistow 33A) often finding their way down, dead in a freight train from Wellingborough.

Brought up on a diet of 'Jubilee' and Stanier and later BR Standard Class '5MT' 4-6-0 locomotives from the depots at Millhouses (Sheffield), Holbeck (Leeds), Trafford Park (Manchester), Kentish Town (London), Derby and Nottingham, they were the standard first line motive power on the expresses to and from St Pancras. Freight traffic was handled by Stanier 2-8-0s and the mighty Beyer-Garratts, soon to be ousted out by the introduction of BR Standard Class '9F' 2-10-0s, the odd 'WD' Austerity plus the multitude of Midland type 0-6-0s, many of which lasted almost until the end of steam in the area.

A feature of the Midland Division had been double-heading, where, south of Derby and Nottingham, pre-war speeds had been fully restored, but with increased loads. A limit of 300 tons tare weight was fixed for 'Jubilee' 4-6-0s on 'XL Limit' timings, but unfortunately, a nine-coach train of standard stock, including a restaurant car, exceeded this figure, so a pilot engine could be called for by the driver of a 'Jubilee' or a 'Black 5' if he was expected to keep time on this schedule. With a Class '2' or '4P' 4-4-0 provided as the pilot engine, one did wonder at times whether this was a hindrance or a help.

In 1955, 'Royal Scot' No. 46120 *Royal Iniskilling Fusilier* had been on loan for twelve weeks to the Mechanical & Electrical Engineers' department at Derby, from where its chief duties were the 7.55am Derby to London (St Pancras) service and the 5.30pm St Pancras to Nottingham duty. This may well have been the prelude to the transfer of six 'Royal Scots' from the Western Division sheds for the 1957 winter timetable. Allocated to Kentish Town (14B), Nos. 46110 *Grenadier Guardsman*, 46116 *Irish Guardsman*, 46127 *Old Contemptibles*, 46131 *The Royal Warwickshire Regiment*, 46152 *The Kings Dragoon Guardsman*, 46157 *The Royal Artilleryman* were put to work on the Manchester route. On 'XL Limit' schedules the 'Royal Scots' were allowed 300 tons between Derby and Manchester, whilst 340 tons applied elsewhere. This effectively reduced the uneconomic double-heading on the Midland lines.

Quite unexpectedly, during the mid-1950s, five Lincoln-allocated former Great Central Railway 'D11' class 4-4-0s began to work through to the Midland lines. The former Midland shed at Lincoln had come under the control of the Eastern Region and, although a small number of London Midland Region engines were still there, most of the through workings between Lincoln and Derby were in the hands of Eastern Region locomotives. In the spring of 1957, five 'D16' class 4-4-0s from Cambridge replaced the 'D11s', which were transferred to Sheffield (Darnall) shed. However, that proved to be a temporary measure as a year later the 'D16s' were themselves replaced by the introduction of diesel-multiple-units on the Derby to Lincoln, Leicester and Nottingham services.

A further reshuffle of express motive power took place in July 1958, when six 'Britannia' Pacifics were procured, Nos. 70004 *William Shakespeare* and 70014 *Iron Duke* from Stewarts Lane, 70015 *Apollo*, 70017 *Arrow*, and 70021 *Morning Star* from Cardiff (Canton) and 70042 *Lord Roberts*

from Stratford; then transferred to the Midland Division and allocated to Trafford Park, Nos. 70004, 70014, 70017 and 70042 initially stopping off at Kentish Town shed for a couple of weeks. This allowed the 'Royal Scots' to be returned from Kentish Town to the Western Division. Three more 'Britannias', Nos. 70031 *Byron*, 70032 *Tennyson* and 70033 *Charles Dickens*, appeared at a later date, bringing the stud of 'Britannias' at Trafford Park to nine.

Motive power was ever changing – late 1959 saw a further batch of '7P' 4-6-0s obtained from the Western Lines by the Midland, with rebuilt 'Patriots' and 'Royal Scots' allocated to Kentish Town, Millhouses and Nottingham. The latter two sheds received their first '7Ps', including No. 46100 *Royal Scot* and the appropriately named No. 46112 *Sherwood Forester* exchanged with Holbeck for Kentish Town's No. 46130, no doubt with a view to it working the 'Robin Hood' – the 8.15am Up service from Nottingham and the corresponding 4.45pm return duty from St Pancras.

Towards the end of 1960, Trafford Park relinquished its 'Britannias' back to the Western Lines as these engines had not taken kindly to regular service over the curves on the Midland, in particular the Derby to Manchester route. Main line diesels were also appearing in ever increasing numbers, and not only from BR Workshops. The Metropolitan-Vickers 'Type 2' Co-Bo 1,200hp units, with a top speed of 75mph, had a short spell operating in pairs on the London (St Pancras) to Manchester (Central) expresses. A pair of these worked a 'Freightliner' trial run from Hendon to Gushetfaulds in Glasgow on 1 October 1958. The service was inaugurated the following March, operating Up on Sundays to Thursdays and in reverse Mondays to Fridays and named 'Condor'. This, the fastest freight train on BR, initially ran with its 27 roller-bearing fitted, vacuum-braked 'Platefit' wagons loaded with containers, and was subjected to the contingency that if one of the Metro-Vick diesels failed before the start of the journey, the orders were that two Class '5' 4-6-0s must be substituted for both diesels, but if a diesel failed *en route*, it could be replaced by a single Class '5', which must be coupled behind the surviving diesel. Also coming on stream around this time were BR/Sulzer Type '4' diesel locomotives, and it would not be long before they would monopolise the working of the expresses on the Midland main line, something they would continue to do until the introduction of HSTs in 1982.

Before leaving Derby, we cross the town – city status was conferred in 1977 – to its other station on the Great Northern Railway, opened as Derby on 1 April 1878 and renamed Derby Friargate three years later. The GNR's Derbyshire and Staffordshire had an extension that linked Nottingham and Grantham to the east and Burton on Trent in the southwest of the area, and the line had such an impact on Derby, Friargate, and the surrounding areas that it became known as the Derby Friargate line. In the 1950s and early 1960s, this ex-GNR/LNER Friargate station was usually used for many popular excursions to the seaside resorts of Skegness, Mablethorpe, Ramsgate and Llandudno. The line became a casualty of the Beeching report and closed to passenger trains on 7 September 1964.

In the summer of 1839, the Midland Counties Railway opened the line from Derby to Nottingham to passenger traffic with four intermediate stations at Borrowash, Breaston, Long Eaton and Beeston, with Spondon opening later that year. To avoid confusion with Beeston, the station at Breaston was re-named Sawley in 1840 – my grandfather was the Stationmaster there when it closed in 1930 – also that year the extension south to Leicester was completed. In 1844, the company amalgamated with the Birmingham & Derby Junction Railway and the North Midland Railway to form the Midland Railway, with Derby – headquarters of the Midland.

In 1847, the Erewash Valley line was opened, and finally the branch line to Stenson Junction providing the connection to Birmingham was instituted in 1873. Further stations on the Derby to Nottingham line were opened, Draycott in 1852, Attenborough in 1864, and Sawley Junction opened in December 1888. With new junctions and the rearrangement of the layout of lines in the vicinity of Trent, the station opened on 1 May 1862, but its original purpose was not to serve Long Eaton; that already had a station at Meadow Lane, which, when closed and demolished, later moved to a more central position in the town. The direct line from there to Platt's crossing became Trent girder yard, with the truncated line from Sawley Junction re-aligned to connect at Trent Station North Junction.

Sir Edmund Beckett, who in the nineteenth century was closely connected with the birth of independent railway companies, wrote of Trent:

'You arrive at Trent, but where that is I cannot tell. I suppose it is somewhere near the River Trent; but then the Trent is a very long river. You get out of your train to obtain refreshments, and having taken them you endeavour to find your train and your carriage. But whether it is on this side or that, and whether it is going north or south, this way or that, you cannot tell. Bewildered, you frantically rush into your carriage; the train moves off round a curve; then you are horrified to see some red lights glaring in front of, and you are in imminent expectation of a collision when your fellow passengers calm your fears by telling you that they are only the tail lamps of your own train!'

Further to the Baron's comments, 'Well, I'll go to Trent', was an expression that my mother would make when she was faced with situations surpassing belief. Trent was a station without a town, 119¾ miles from London (St Pancras) on the former Midland Railway lines of the London Midland Region of British Railways. Sited in the south-east corner of Derbyshire, the county town was situated just over nine miles to the west, and Nottingham just under seven miles to the east. The River Trent, the third longest river in England, from which the station took its name, runs nearby. Trent station was nineteenth century some might say, one of the cornerstones of the Midland Railway Empire. Of Midland Railway Gothic architecture with a honeycomb of cellars and interlinking upper storeys, Trent's position and importance was as an interchange junction for five main railway routes, through its plethora of junctions, serving Nottingham, Derby, Birmingham, Chesterfield and the City of London. Remarkably enough, trains could depart from opposite platforms in opposite directions to the same destination.

The station was a sizeable one with its single island platform; it included booking hall, waiting rooms, refreshment room, bookstall, train crew relief cabin and a ticket barrier that was manned on the early and late turns. This issued either a platform ticket, or a ticket to purchase a ticket to travel at the booking office. The Signal & Telegraph department had a room at platform level, whilst the Permanent Way Inspector's office was located upstairs. The station site was surrounded only by an isolated farm, a cottage that was linked to a rifle range, the Stationmaster's house, and ten railway cottages. With no buses passing the station entrance, and no taxi rank, many would-be passengers opted for 'Shank's pony' as a means of getting to the station, either by using the 600 yards of sparsely gas-lit footpath from North Erewash Junction, or by the longer route down Meadow Lane and over Long Eaton Junction level crossing.

Each day, nearly 100 passenger and parcels trains called at Trent station, with very few passenger trains not stopping there. Local services were in the hands of ex-Midland Class '2P' & '4P' 4-4-0s or Fowler and Stanier 2-6-4Ts, supplemented by the odd Class '4F' 0-6-0 with archaic non-corridor coaches on workmen's services, those then giving way to diesel-multiple-units operating between Derby, Nottingham and Lincoln, as well as between Nottingham, Leicester and Birmingham. The two routes connected

at Trent to provide an interval service between Derby and Leicester that supplemented the Manchester to London (St Pancras) expresses. The principle expresses from St Pancras, those to Manchester, generally avoided running via Trent station, whilst the services to Leeds and Bradford, and also the 'Thames-Clyde Express', were routed through the station, initially to eschew the conurbations of Derby and Nottingham, from where connecting services were in place for the transfer of passengers.

At the turn of the century there were two rows of trees on each side of the station, and those on the north side are extant today, despite the remodelling of the junction when the station closed from New Year's Day 1968 and the building of an adjacent industrial estate, whilst those on the south side were felled to allow the construction of the high-level goods lines into Toton. These allowed the intensive goods workings to avoid Trent station and also the two busy level crossings in later years on the Erewash Valley line at Long Eaton; the high-level lines carried the heaviest freight traffic in the country and remain in use today.

Toton, with its large Railway Depot and Marshalling Yard was situated on the southern fringe of the Nottinghamshire and Derbyshire coalfield on the Trent to Chesterfield (Erewash Valley) line. About two miles north of Trent, it was an important section of the former Midland Railway and formed part of one of the main trunk routes between London and the North. The Motive Power Depot at Toton (18A) purportedly became the largest freight engine shed on the London Midland & Scottish Railway. Passenger trains over this route were in the minority, notably the 'Thames-Clyde Express', a St Pancras to Bradford Forster Square express – of which there were two in the reverse direction, until diverted over the Trowell branch into Nottingham and running via Melton Mowbray – and a Nottingham to Sheffield local service serving stations along the Erewash Valley.

Toton Sidings were originally developed in the 1850s, getting the name from the small village to the east of the Yard. During the years up to the turn of the nineteenth century, there was unprecedented growth, principally in coal output leading to the expansion of Toton Sidings as a major marshalling yard. Being a 'flat type' yard, the wagons were shunted into place, not only by locomotives, but also using horses.

Frederick S. Williams, a minister in the Congregational Church, and renowned nineteenth century railway historian, best known for his books on the early history of the railway, wrote in his 1883 version of *Our Iron Roads*:

'The amount of business done at Toton day and night is enormous, but it varies with the season. In a summer month 18,000 wagons will be received and despatched; in winter as many as 26,000. The staff required also depends on the season and the work. In summer perhaps thirty or forty shunting horses would suffice, but in a severe winter the grease in the axle box will freeze hard, the wheels instead of turning round will skid along the rails, and two or three horses will be required to move a wagon. It is very interesting to see their sagacity and to watch them picking their way among the moving wagons, especially at night. After being suddenly unhooked from a wagon they will be perfectly still where there is just room for them to stand between two lines of rails, while a squealing engine and a shunt of wagons passes on each side of them. It used to be said that there were a great many accidents. Sir Beckett Denison, in one of his kind speeches, called Toton sidings the Midland Company's "slaughter house" – didn't he?'

The sidings comprised of two marshalling yards, the Up on the east side and the Down on the west side of the main running lines extending over a distance of nearly two miles between Stapleford & Sandiacre and Long Eaton passenger and goods stations. The Up yard was used as an assembling point for wagons conveying coal from Nottinghamshire, Derbyshire and South Yorkshire coalfields, and as a sorting and despatching point mainly to London and the South, Birmingham and the West, Peterborough and the Eastern counties. The Down yard was used principally for sorting empty mineral wagons in the reverse direction, en route to the collieries. At both yards, incoming trains were broken up and the wagons sorted for different destinations and directions.

A total of thirty-three Garratts were built by Beyer, Peacock & Co Ltd for the London, Midland & Scottish Railway, the first three appearing in 1927, the remainder delivered in the latter part of 1930. The class was allocated to Toton, Hasland and Wellingborough for the movement of coal to the south and west, as well as for the working of iron-ore from the Northamptonshire fields to the north-east. Prior to the introduction of the main batch of Beyer-Garratts, coal train workings between Toton and Brent used double-headed Class '3F' and '4F' 0-6-0s.

London and the Home Counties had an insatiable appetite for coal and many of the enormous Brent-bound trains were marshalled at Stanton Gate Up Sidings, a mile to the north of Toton; these were despatched often hourly, with a change of crew at either Sandiacre or Toton Centre. Driver William (Bill) Webb of Toton motive power depot fondly recalled his footplate experiences, in particular with the mighty Beyer-Garratts, a locomotive that he positively revered. As he explained, he liked nothing better than running bunker-first, where he could sit with his feet up without smoke and steam enveloping the cab and obscuring the sighting of signals. Some fastidious drivers however, did not agree and they would insist on the engine being turned before working the train. As there was no turntable on the system that was large enough to accommodate these locomotives, they had to be turned on the triangle at Trent, or at Cricklewood at the London end of the line. In 1931, the Toton Local Departmental Committee submitted a complaint on behalf of enginemen working the Garratt engines tender first, which was declined by the Company's representatives.

As a postscript to the Beyer-Garratts, Bill would occasionally reflect on an incident when the driver and fireman were badly scalded when a steam pipe burst over the fire. After discussing this with George Bailey – I was his box lad in 1957 – he must have given the matter some thought and wrote to me:

'While working at Toton East Junction Signal Box during the winter of 1940, Garratt engine No. 7967 was taking a coal train from Sandiacre (it had been worked to that point from Stanton Gate) to Brent on a Sunday night. As the train passed the box, both the driver – W. Hurley, and the locomotive's fireman Punch Wooley, who had taken over from the booked fireman, who was sick – could be seen firing the locomotive. When the train got to Ratcliffe Junction, some three miles into its journey, a boiler pipe burst over the fire. Both footplatemen were severely scalded. The driver stopped the train and assisted the fireman to walk back to the guard. The guard is recorded as carrying both enginemen some distance in an attempt to save their lives. The footplate crew were eventually taken to Loughborough hospital, but died later. To make matters worse there was a severe frost at the time.'

In an attempt to expedite the movement of coal from colliery to customers, 'improving the flow', in particular to the capital, a programme of high-speed Fitted Coal Train Tests between Toton and Brent was undertaken during late 1951, and continued until 1955 using motive power not normally associated with such work.

A pair of 'Royal Scots', Nos. 46117 *Welsh Guardsman* and 46154 *The Hussar,* were tried in November 1951 and after that a brace of Stanier 'Black Fives', Nos. 44667 and 45342, worked a train of fifty-two vacuum-fitted wagons and a dynamometer car over the same route in January 1952; there were tests with other locomotive types too in the same period. Later, a couple of BR Standard

Class '5MTs', Nos. 73000 and 73001, entered the fray and Nos. 73030 and 73031 also had a share of the spoils. Lastly, a pair of 2-10-0 Class '9Fs' were utilised.

On 20 January 1952, drivers William Webb and Stan Woods were paired together to work 'The Flying Collier'. BR 'Britannia' Pacifics, Nos. 70020 *Mercury* and 70023 Venus, had been borrowed from Old Oak Common (81A) to work the special test train hauling seventy 16 ton loaded wagons and a dynamometer car from Toton to Brent. An account of the run appeared in the March edition of *Coal - The Magazine of the Mining Industry*

In addition to the Toton to Brent fitted coal train tests, others were run as far as Bedford in December of that year, on that occasion, hauling fifty-two 16ton empty wagons, and Toton driver William Webb had charge of BR Standard Class '5MT' 4-6-0 No. 73031. Static tests were also undertaken on the Erewash Valley by the Derby Research Department, where the Westinghouse Brake Trials necessitated the complete occupation of No. 2 Down Goods line between Trowell Junction and Ilkeston South Junction, which also produced a varied selection of motive power including those aforementioned – and in 1953 two ex-LNER 'L1' Class 2-6-4Ts Nos. 67729 and 67737, were appropriated from Stratford for the purpose.

Leaving the Erewash Valley line, onward through Beeston to Nottingham and its environs, where the Midland station, first built by the Midland Railway in 1848, and rebuilt by them in 1904 when Albert Edward Lambert, a local Nottingham architect was appointed. Lambert had been the architect for the Nottingham Victoria railway station and consequently the two buildings shared many similarities in their design. For many years, the Midland Railway suffered the indignity of its rival, the Great Central Railway, crossing above the station on a 170-foot-long (52m) bowstring girder bridge. This bridge became redundant in 1973 and was finally dismantled in the early 1980s. The alignment was later used for a new tramway bridge built on top of part of the old Great Central main line viaduct. Nottingham station was partially closed for ten weeks during 2013 for track and signalling work.

Of all the major new main line routes built in the nineteenth century, the Great Central seems to attract the most attention, since the London Extension line was the last to be built. Nottingham Victoria railway station was a Great Northern Railway and Great Central Railway station opened on 24 May 1900 by the Nottingham Joint Station Committee.

The nationalisation of the railways in 1948 led to the Great Central metals becoming part of the Eastern Region of British Railways. In 1958, the ex-Great Central route was allocated to the Midland Region of British Railways and so were sown the seeds of its decline as a main line to London. The Midland region was staffed by members of the former Midland Railway who had been bitter rivals of the Great Central.

On summer Saturdays in 1959, overnight outward services included:

10pm (Friday) Sheffield Victoria-Portsmouth Harbour arrive 4.13am

11.30pm (Friday) Nottingham Victoria-Portsmouth Harbour arrive 4.23am

1.0am Leicester Central-Margate/Ramsgate arrive 6.19am

11.35pm (Friday) Derby Friargate-Ramsgate arrive 6.51am (Until 15 September)

11.40pm (Friday) Sheffield Victoria-Hastings arrive 7.35am (4 July to 29 August)

10.22pm (Friday) York-Swindon arrive 5.45am

2.45am Nottingham Victoria-Bournemouth Central arrive 8.16am

5.20am Leicester Central-Llandudno arrive 10.54am (4 July to 10 September)

7.45am Leicester-Scarborough Londesborough Road arrive 1.25pm (Runs 20 June, 29 August, 5 September)

8.25am Leicester-Scarborough Londesborough Road arrive 1.25pm (27 June to 22 August)

10.15am Bradford-Poole arrive 6.20pm

8.35am Newcastle-Bournemouth West arrive 6.53pm

12.10pm Sheffield Victoria-Bournemouth Central arrive 7.16pm

10.08 Newcastle-Swansea High Street arrive 9.10pm

5.30pm Scarborough-Swindon arrive 2.0am (11 July to 12 September)

'Starlight Specials', cheap excursion trains, ran from London to Glasgow and Edinburgh; these were overnight services that ran during the summer months and were routed over both the Midland and Great Central lines and were well patronised. Another summer service train was the Marylebone-Stirling car-sleeper service.

During the early 1960s, diverting services to other routes was a deliberate ploy on behalf of the British Railways Board in cognisance with the forthcoming Beeching Report in running down many of the lines across the country, which included the whole Great Central route. The rundown of the GCR was inevitable as traffic was transferred to the former Midland route. Locomotives, most in a poor mechanical condition were unreliable and old; the line did not benefit from British Rail's new diesel locomotives and had become a last haven for redundant steam locomotives, offering them a brief respite before being summoned to the scrap yards. People were using other forms of transport including the motor car; passenger numbers were falling and closure seemed inevitable. Country stations such as those at Belgrave & Birstall, Rothley and Quorn & Woodhouse were closed in 1963. This once proud line that only a few years earlier furnished services to almost all parts of England, Wales and Scotland did so without encountering a single level crossing from Beighton Junction (Sheffield) through to London (Marylebone),.

Freight traffic through Nottingham Victoria station was varied with trains carrying a variety of merchandise including fish from Hull and Grimsby for South Wales and Plymouth. The infamous Annesley to Woodford trains initially worked by a selection of ex-GC or L&NE locomotives but in the late fifties by BR Standard 2-10-0 '9Fs', nicknamed 'Runners' and 'Windcutters'. These tightly timed trains were purported to be the fastest out-and-home loose coupled freight service in the country.

Through expresses were withdrawn in 1960 with a very poor semi-fast service introduced between Nottingham and London, the last passenger train leaving Nottingham Victoria for Marylebone at 17.15 on 3 September 1966 hauled by Stanier Class '5' No. 44984. The line closed as a through route to London and the line was severed just south of Rugby and was closed on 4 September 1967 by the London Midland Region of British Railways, as was the once elegant station at Nottingham Victoria although goods trains continued to pass through the site of Victoria until May 1968, with two running lines left in place amidst the demolition of the main station.

Although main line services had ceased, the section between Rugby and Nottingham was retained for a commuter service using diesel-multiple-units terminating at Arkwright Street. This service was not without its problems; reliability was poor, as I know from first-hand experience as a DMU Controller at Furlong House at the time. The early morning service from Rugby had late starts and cancellations owing to flat batteries and other defects on the DMUs. The service would cease on 3 May 1969, when the ex-GC line south of the city closed to passenger traffic.

British Railways came into being in 1948, and to avoid confusion the two Melton stations were renamed Melton Town and Melton North in 1950 but it was clear that passenger traffic on the Great Northern and London and North Western Joint Railway was not sufficient to justify keeping the stations on the route open and Melton North closed to all passenger traffic other than holiday excursions in the summer on 5 December 1953. The last holiday excursion ran on 9 September 1962, though goods traffic remained heavy, keeping the station yard busy until complete closure on 29 May 1964.

The Midland Railway and the Great Northern Joint Railway, (M&GN) affectionately known as the 'Muddle and Get Nowhere' to generations of passengers, enthusiasts and other users, gets its name from the two older companies which owned it. With Grouping in 1923, the M&GN became jointly owned by the London and North Eastern Railway (LNER) and the London, Midland and Scottish Railway (LMS), but it retained its own identity and operated much as it had before the Grouping. Much of the route was single-track and the gradient profiles were steep. The main thrust of M&GN services was to and from the Midlands. Saxby became a junction when the Midland and Great Northern Railway (M&GN) opened on 1 May 1894 and the station closed on 6 February 1961.

The M & GN Joint line emanated from Saxby on the Midland Railway's Melton route and from Peterborough on the Great Northern Railway's East Coast mainline, uniting at Sutton Bridge East Junction to enter Norfolk and run eastwards via South Lynn and Melton Constable. Here, at Melton Constable, where a locomotive works was situated, the Joint Line split three ways to reach Norwich, Cromer and Great Yarmouth. Each of these locations had stations separate from the rival Great Eastern Railway.

After nationalisation in 1948, the M&GN looked vulnerable; few passenger trains ran on the Joint, except on summer Saturdays when numerous holiday trains from the East Midland conurbations placed much demand on line capacity. The single track (approximately 60 per cent of the route mileage), although operated by the most up-to-date methods (the electric train tablet system) did make the seasonal peak loads difficult to handle – August Bank Holiday weekends were particularly difficult, with waves of special trains from and to the Midlands having to thread their way through the normal traffic of local trains and freights. The goods traffic was also very heavy, particularly coal inwards, and fruit, vegetables, other agricultural products and fish outwards. As well as local traffic, the M&GN created a series of regular long-distance services, linking, for example, London King's Cross to Cromer, with regular daily services from Liverpool, Manchester, Nottingham, Leeds, Birmingham and Leicester to South Lynn, Cromer, Norwich and Great Yarmouth.

When the Midland and Great Northern line closed in March 1959, it was the biggest wholesale closure of the system to date, with 180 miles of track serving sixty-five stations and halts, some of which were only open in the summer with displaced traffic mostly transferring to the former GER routes.

Throughout its years of operation under many different owners, and notwithstanding the high proportion of its route that was single-track, it was an extremely safe system – not a single passenger was killed on the M&GN.

The *Railway Gazette* reported in its April 1959 edition – 'Midlands to Norfolk via March':

'Accelerations of up to 96 minutes eastbound and 87 minutes westbound in holiday trains at weekends this summer between the Midlands and East Anglian coast resorts are justification for closing most of the Midland & Great Northern line at the end of February. Trains from Rugby, Leicester, and other stations in the Midlands to the Norfolk coast resorts will be routed via March and the Ely avoiding line, by the Great Eastern route. The absence of the MGN line and the extension of non-stop running have facilitated the cuts in journey times. Because access to Yarmouth, Cromer, and Sheringham is now from the south, via Norwich (or Trowse curve), the distances between those resorts and the Midlands are increased by 10, 41, and 49 miles respectively, but the westbound from Sheringham there will be some accelerations compared with the old M&GN route.'

The Midland main line from Kettering to Nottingham closed to passenger traffic on 1 May 1967 – the few expresses to and from London St Pancras were routed via Leicester – and totally as a through route on 4 November 1968, but it was retained as far as Edwalton as the Old Dalby test track, meaning that Melton Junction remains on the railway map.

Changing engines on long distance trains at intermediate stations became quite common in the 1950s to balance crew workings. On the Midland Division, Kentish Town's engine and crews worked throughout the 190 mile journey to Manchester Central. Locomotives from Barrow Road shed worked through from Bristol to Leeds whilst those to Newcastle had an engine change at Sheffield or York. At Carlisle on the West Coast main line, the 'Princess Coronation Class' locomotives from Polmadie shed were changed for one of the 'Duchesses' from Upperby, Crewe or Camden sheds.

On the East Coast route, long-distance engine workings to Leeds and Newcastle had been introduced around 1950 to balance crew workings. However, because of poor engine performance, the through engine workings were reduced to a minimum again and the former practice of changing engines on long distance trains at various intermediate stations, Peterborough, Grantham, Doncaster and York, was by and large restored by 1956-57. Grantham continued to be an important change-over point where expresses exchanged engines and features in the final part of this book; the depot closed in September 1963. Indeed, the 'A4' Pacific reserve locomotive from Top Shed for the 'Elizabethan' non-stop express was invariably put to work on the 'Northumbrian', 12.18pm Kings Cross to Newcastle duty as far as Grantham, the locomotive then returning on an express to London, thereby ensuring its availability for standby duty at Kings Cross the following day.

CHAPTER 1

DERBY MIDLAND STATION

Johnson 4-4-0 Class '2P' No. 40383 is on station pilot duty at Derby on 19 January 1952. It was built in 1888 at the nearby Works and disposed of there when withdrawn from Derby shed six months after this photograph was taken. *(M.E. Kirk/Martyn Reeve Collection)*

Headboard being affixed prior to the start of the Derby District S.L.S. Rail Tour, worked by Johnson Midland 0-4-4T Class '1P' No. 58087 at Derby station on 28 June 1952. It was built in 1900 by Dubs & Co. and condemned in June 1955 from Plaistow shed and disposed of at Derby Works. *(M.E. Kirk/Martyn Reeve Collection)*

The 10.20am Bristol (Temple Meads) to Newcastle (Central) express is ready to depart from Derby station behind ex-LMS 'Black Five' No. 44858 on 3 July 1954. It was built in 1944 at Crewe Works and withdrawn in December 1967 from Carlisle (Kingmoor) shed and scrapped at T.W. Ward Killamarsh. A modernisation plan was under way which involved the demolition of the Stephenson train shed. Extensive rebuilding of the platform buildings, footbridge and awnings was put in hand in 1952, using pre-stressed concrete, which gave the station a very different appearance. *(M.E. Kirk/Martyn Reeve Collection)*

Fowler 0-6-0T Class '3F' No. 47485 on station pilot duties at Derby on 5 March 1955. Built in 1928 at the Vulcan Foundry, it was withdrawn from Edge Hill shed in January 1965 and cut up by Maden & McKee, Liverpool. *(M.E. Kirk/Martyn Reeve Collection)*

Sneaking through the goods lines at Derby Midland station on 5 March 1955 is Johnson Midland 0-6-0 Class '3F' No. 43572 on a short freight train, waiting patiently in a blustery north wind for the signal to be cleared. Built in 1899 by Kitson, it was withdrawn in November 1960 from Trafford Park shed and scrapped at Crewe Works. *(M.E. Kirk/Martyn Reeve Collection)*

Often referred to as 'Flying Pigs', Ivatt 2-6-0 Class '4' No. 43041 is about to depart from Derby station with the 12.10pm to Lincoln (St Marks) on 5 March 1955. Built in 1949 at Horwich Works and withdrawn from Lostock Hall shed in August 1967, it was disposed of at Clayton & Davie, Dunston-on-Tyne. The leading two coaches are Midland railway stock. *(M.E. Kirk/Martyn Reeve Collection)*

Seen here from platform 6 at Derby station on 5 March 1955, probably heading to Chaddesden sidings are Hughes 2-6-0 '6P5F' No. 42822, built in 1929 at Horwich Works and broken up there when withdrawn from Burton shed in June 1962, coupled to Fowler 0-6-0 '4F' No. 44212, built in 1925 at Derby Works and withdrawn in December 1963 from Staveley (Barrow Hill) shed and cut up by T.W.Ward, Killamarsh: Compound No. 41185 waits for the road at Engine Siding No 1 signal box; a product from the Vulcan Foundry in 1927 and condemned from Derby shed in October 1957 and scrapped at the adjacent Works. *(M.E. Kirk/Martyn Reeve Collection)*

The Running Foreman at Kentish Town has appropriated Holbeck's long-term resident, 'Jubilee' 4-6-0 Class '6P' No. 45675 *Hardy* to work a London (St Pancras)-Manchester (Central) express on 5 March 1955, having just taken on water at Derby station. Built in 1935 at Crewe Works and withdrawn from Holbeck shed in June 1967, it was disposed of at Cashmore's, Great Bridge. *(M.E. Kirk/Martyn Reeve Collection)*

Burton-allocated Johnson 4-4-0 Class '2P' No. 40364 waiting to leave platform 3 at the London Road Junction end of Derby station, probably for Birmingham New Street with a local stopping train on 5 March 1955. Built in 1886 at Derby Works, it was cut up there when condemned from Burton shed after just over seventy years in service. *(M.E. Kirk/Martyn Reeve Collection)*

Known as the *Tutbury Jinny,* Riddles BR Standard 2-6-2T Class '2' No. 84006 waits to leave Tutbury station for Burton-on-Trent on 2 June 1956. Built in 1953 at Crewe Works and withdrawn twelve years later from Leicester shed, it was scrapped at Buttigiegs, Newport. *(M.E. Kirk/Martyn Reeve Collection)*

Viewed from platform 6 at Derby station at 8.30pm on 12 June 1955 is a line-up of Fowler locomotives. 4-4-0 'Compound' No. 41119, built in 1925 at Horwich Works and withdrawn from Leeds (Holbeck) shed in December 1958 was broken up at T.W.Ward, Killamarsh. 2-6-4T Class '4P' No. 42410, built in 1933 at Derby Works and withdrawn in September 1966 from Huddersfield shed, was cut up at Cashmore's, Great Bridge. 'Compound' No. 40917, built in 1927 at the Vulcan Foundry and condemned from Bournville shed in December 1956, was scrapped at Derby Works. 0-6-0 Class '4F' No. 44096 built in 1925 by Kerr Stuart, it was condemned in September 1964 from Gorton shed and disposed of at Cohens, Ickles. In the rear is Fowler 2-6-4T No. 42347 & Fowler No. 44560, ex-Somerset & Dorset Joint Railway. *(M.E. Kirk/Martyn Reeve Collection)*

A grimy Johnson 4-4-0 Class '2P' No. 40416 is shown here on station pilot duty at Derby on 2 July 1955. Built in 1892 by Sharp, Stewart and Company, it was withdrawn in May 1959 from Derby shed and disposed of at Crewe Works. *(M.E. Kirk/Martyn Reeve Collection)*

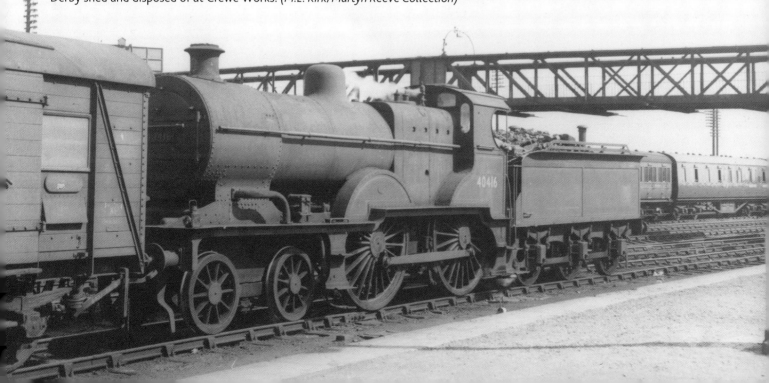

The 10.50am (Sun) Derby to Crewe stopping train waits on platform 2 on 15 April 1956 and is being worked by Fowler 2-6-4T Class '4P' No. 42316. It was built in 1928 at Derby Works and scrapped there when withdrawn from Stockport (Edgeley) shed in February 1963. *(M.E. Kirk/Martyn Reeve Collection)*

The wheeltapper at Derby station is seen here doing his rounds on 15 April 1956 with the 9.45am (Sun) Nottingham-Buxton stopping train hauled by Hughes 2-6-0 Class '6P5F' No. 42847, built in 1930 at Horwich Works and broken up there when condemned from Gorton shed in June 1962. The second coach is L&YR M15239M. Compare earlier 1954 photo of the station train shed (image page 18) with that of 44858. *(M.E. Kirk/Martyn Reeve Collection)*

The **5.15pm Derby** to Worcester (Shrub Hill) stopping train with Midland 4-4-0 Class '2P' No. 40511 in charge simmers gently on platform 4 on 12 May 1956. Built in 1899 by Sharp, Stewart and Company and withdrawn in January 1961 from Toton shed, it was scrapped at Albert Loom, Spondon. *(M.E. Kirk/Martyn Reeve Collection)*

With platform resurfacing in progress under the reinforced concrete pillars and beams, the 1.05pm (SO) Derby-Manchester (Central) stopping train headed by Fowler (3-Cyl. Compound) Class '4P' No. 40927 is about to depart from platform 2 on 21 April 1956. Built in 1927 at the Vulcan Foundry, it was withdrawn from Derby shed in July 1957 and broken up at the nearby Works. *(M.E. Kirk/Martyn Reeve Collection)*

Derby station on 25 April 1956, ex-LMS Stanier 4-6-0 No. 44830 piloted by Fowler Class '2P' No. 40682 are in charge of the 8.30am Cardiff-Newcastle express. The 'Black Five' was built in 1944 at Crewe Works and withdrawn from Heaton Mersey shed in August 1967 and disposed of at T.W.Ward, Beighton. 40682 was built in 1932 at Derby Works and condemned from Nottingham shed in February 1961 and disposed of by Albert Loom, Spondon. On platform 2 is the 1.05pm (SO) to Manchester (Central) with Fowler 'Compound' No. 40927, which emerged in 1927 from the Vulcan Foundry, was withdrawn from Derby shed in July 1957 and broken up at the nearby Works. *(M.E. Kirk/Martyn Reeve Collection)*

Seen here leaving the station after attaching the pilot engine, Fowler 4-4-0 Class '2P' No. 40682 and Stanier Class '5' No. 44830 working the **8.30am** Cardiff to Newcastle express on 25 April 1956. *(M.E. Kirk/Martyn Reeve Collection)*

The 5.48pm Derby-Nottingham workman's stopping train, which was routed out of the north end of the station and ran via Chaddesden, is headed by Robinson 4-4-0 'Director' Class 'D11' No. 62667 *Somme* on 12 May 1956. It was built in 1922 at Gorton Works and condemned in August 1960 from Sheffield (Darnall) shed, later disposed of at Doncaster Works. *(M.E. Kirk/Martyn Reeve Collection)*

The shed foreman at Derby is making full use of 'foreign' motive power at his disposal on Good Friday in April 1957. Carlisle (Upperby)-allocated 4-6-0 'Black Five' No. 45371 is appropriated to work the 1.45pm local train to Birmingham. An Armstrong Whitworth product of 1937, it was withdrawn from Workington shed in April 1967 and broken up at Motherwell Machinery & Scrap, Wishaw. Leeds (Holbeck) 'Black Five' No. 44757 fitted with Caprotti valve gear is on the 2.10pm departure to Crewe; built in 1948 at Crewe Works and withdrawn from Brunswick shed in November 1965, it was cut up at Cashmore's, Great Bridge. *(M.E. Kirk/Martyn Reeve Collection)*

Johnson 4-4-0 Class '2P' 40404, its MR tender complete with coal rails, is on station pilot duty at Derby over Easter in 1957. Manufactured in 1892 by Sharp, Stewart and Company, Glasgow and with just three months left in traffic when this picture was taken, it was condemned from Derby shed after sixty-five years in service and scrapped at the nearby Works. *(M.E. Kirk/Martyn Reeve Collection)*

Fairburn 2-6-4T Class '4MT' 42174 brings the empty-stock into the station for the 2.05pm Derby-Rowsley excursion on Good Friday 19 April 1957. Built in 1948 at Derby Works and withdrawn in August 1965 from Springs Branch (Wigan) shed, disposal was at Cashmore's, Newport. *(M.E. Kirk/Martyn Reeve Collection)*

Another 1957 Good Friday visitor at Derby Midland station, Stanier 4-6-0 Class '5' No. 45440 from Bath Green Park shed leaves with a 2.30pm special to Gloucester. An Armstrong Whitworth 1937 build, the locomotive was withdrawn from Edge Hill shed in September 1967 and broken up at Cashmore's, Newport. *(M.E. Kirk/Martyn Reeve Collection)*

On 14 September 1957, BR Standard 4-6-0 Class '5MT' No. 73030 has arrived with the 8.35am Bristol-Newcastle express. Built in 1953 at Derby Works and withdrawn after only 12 years in service from Oxford shed, it was cut up at Cashmore's, Newport. Johnson 4-4-0 Class '2P' No. 40537 of Hasland shed has been attached as pilot; built in 1899 at Derby Works and scrapped there when withdrawn in September 1962 from Templecombe shed. *(M.E. Kirk/Martyn Reeve Collection)*

Another Johnson Midland design and Fowler rebuild, 4-4-0 Class '2P' No. 40493 has arrived with the 9.20am Lincoln-Derby semi-fast on 14 September 1957. Built in 1897 at the nearby Works, this was condemned from Nottingham shed in July 1959 and cut up by T.W.Ward, Killamarsh. *(M.E. Kirk/Martyn Reeve Collection)*

On 16 May 1959, Fowler 2-6-4T Class '4' No. 42326 is performing shunting duties. Built in 1929 at Derby Works, it was broken up there when withdrawn in July 1960 from Gorton shed. The leading vehicle is a GNSR bogie van E7143E. *(M.E. Kirk/Martyn Reeve Collection)*

The 12.48pm York-Bristol express leaves the station behind 'Jubilee' 4-6-0 Class '6P' No. 45660 *Rooke* on 16 May 1959. Built in 1934 at Derby Works and withdrawn from Leeds (Holbeck) shed in July 1966, it was disposed of at Drapers, Hull. *(M.E. Kirk/Martyn Reeve Collection)*

On the same day, 'The Palatine', 2.25pm Manchester (Central)-London (St Pancras) is seen here leaving platform 6 headed by 'Britannia' Pacific No. 70017 *Arrow*. Built in 1951 at Crewe Works, it was withdrawn in October 1966 from Carlisle (Kingmoor) shed and scrapped at Cashmore's, Newport. *(M.E. Kirk/Martyn Reeve Collection)*

Also in May 1959, an up Goods train plods along hauled by Fowler 0-6-0 Class '4F' No. 44419, built in 1927 at Derby Works and condemned from Saltley shed in September 1963 and cut up at Central Wagon Co., Wigan. *(M.E. Kirk/Martyn Reeve Collection)*

The 2.52pm semi-fast from Lincoln (St Marks) passing London Road Junction signal box behind Thompson 4-6-0 'B1' No. 61009 *Hartebeeste* on 16 May 1959, built in 1944 at Darlington Works and withdrawn in September 1962 from Lincoln shed and broken up by Cox & Danks, Wadsley Bridge. *(M.E. Kirk/Martyn Reeve Collection)*

On 9 September 1961, the 1.20pm Darlington to Birmingham express leaves platform 6 behind Gresley 2-6-0 Class 'K3' No. 61989, built in 1937 at Darlington Works and withdrawn from Staveley shed in June 1962 and cut-up at Doncaster Works. *(M.E. Kirk/Martyn Reeve Collection)*

Kentish Town-allocated 'Royal Scot' 4-6-0 Class '7P' No. 46140 *The King's Royal Rifle Corps* before being re-allocated to Newton Heath the following month, stands on platform 1 at Derby station working the 8.40am Bristol-Newcastle express on 19 August 1961. Manufactured by the North British Locomotive Company, Glasgow in 1927, it was withdrawn in October 1965 from Carlisle (Kingmoor) shed and scrapped at J. McWilliams, Shettleston. *(M.E. Kirk/Martyn Reeve Collection)*

On the same morning, 'Jubilee' 4-6-0 Class '6P' No. 45648 *Wemyss* arrives in the rain with a relief train 1X68 from the West Country and the enginemen decide to take on water. Built in 1935 at Crewe Works, it was broken up there when withdrawn from Burton shed in February 1963. *(M.E. Kirk/Martyn Reeve Collection)*

Later that morning, the rain has stopped as Stanier 4-6-0 Class '5' No. 45264 arrives with 1T10 a Leicester-Manchester (Central) excursion train with eleven coaches. An Armstrong Whitworth 1936 build, condemned in September 1967 from Crewe South shed, it was scrapped at Cashmore's, Great Bridge. *(M.E. Kirk/Martyn Reeve Collection)*

With just fifteen months left in service, 'Royal Scot' 4-6-0 Class '7P' No. 46137 *The Prince of Wales's Volunteers (South Lancashire)* departs from platform 6 in August 1961 with 1V41 relief train, 7.38am Sunderland to Birmingham. Built in 1927 by the NBL Co. Glasgow and withdrawn from Carlisle (Upperby) in November 1962, it was scrapped at Crewe Works. *(M.E. Kirk/Martyn Reeve Collection)*

On 12 May 1962, the 7.35am Nottingham to Bristol Temple Meads is on platform 2 at Derby station having arrived via Chaddesden, thus avoiding reversal, hauled by 'Royal Scot' 4-6-0 Class '7P' No. 46141 *The North Staffordshire Regiment* recently allocated to Saltley shed. *(M.E. Kirk/Martyn Reeve Collection)*

Easing the 7.35am Nottingham-Bristol out of platform 2 is 'Royal Scot' 4-6-0 Class '7P' No. 46141 *The North Staffordshire Regiment* in May 1962, manufactured in 1927 by the North British Locomotive Co. Glasgow and withdrawn from Carlisle (Upperby) shed in April 1964 and cut up at Crewe Works. *(M.E. Kirk/Martyn Reeve Collection)*

Fairburn 2-6-4T Class '4P' No. 42174 is on station pilot duty in June 1962. Built in 1948 at Derby Works, it was condemned in August 1965 from Springs Branch (Wigan) shed and broken up at Cashmore's, Newport. *(M.E. Kirk/Martyn Reeve Collection)*

CHAPTER 2

DERBY SHED/ WORKS YARD

Park 0-4-2ST No. 58865, photographed on 18 May 1952 having travelled from Devons Road (Bow) shed to Derby Locomotive Works, is an engine that had achieved a near-century record of continuous service, the 0-4-2 crane engine No. 58865, only representative of its class, which had been condemned after a life of 93 years. Built in 1858, No. 37 of the North London Railway, as she at first was, worked passenger trains between South Acton and Hammersmith. In 1872 she was rebuilt by Sharp Stewart & Co. as a crane engine, renumbered 29, and became the works shunter at Bow, where she continued throughout the rest of her working life. *(M.E. Kirk/Martyn Reeve Collection)*

Whitelegg 4-4-2T Class '2P' No. 41925, built in 1903 by the North British Locomotive Co. Glasgow and condemned from Nottingham shed in April 1952, a month before this image was taken and broken up at Derby Works. *(M.E. Kirk/Martyn Reeve Collection)*

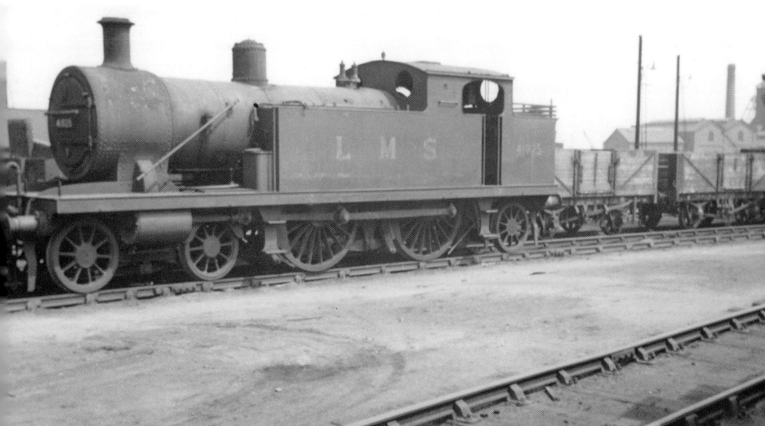

Johnson 4-4-0 Class '2P' No. 40326 is fully coaled with fire-irons visible on 15 April 1956, built in 1921 at Derby Works and condemned the following month after this picture was taken. Behind is Fowler 0-6-0T No. 47293, freshly outshopped from the adjacent Works. *(M.E. Kirk/Martyn Reeve Collection)*

A pair of Johnson 0-6-0Ts on shed on 12 May 1956, No. 41773 built at Derby Works in 1890 and scrapped there when withdrawn in June 1960 from Derby shed, and No. 41724, built in 1882 at Derby Works and condemned from Derby shed in June 1958 and cut up at Crewe Works. *(M.E. Kirk/Martyn Reeve Collection)*

On 12 May 1956, new from Crewe Works less than a fortnight earlier, is Riddles 2-10-0 Class '9F' No. 92079, a replacement for the famous ex-Midland Railway 'Lickey Banker' 0-10-0 No. 58100 *Big Bertha,* fitted with the 0-10-0s large headlamp which was used to help coupling up at night. The '9F' was withdrawn in November 1967 from Birkenhead shed and cut up at Campbell's, Airdrie. Alongside is 'Black Five' No. 44846, built in 1944 at Crewe Works and withdrawn from Newton Heath shed in January 1968 and cut up at Drapers, Hull. *(M.E. Kirk/Martyn Reeve Collection)*

Ex-Lickey Banker, Fowler 0-10-0 *Big Bertha* No. 58100, built in 1919 at Derby Works, pictured here on 12 May 1956 and condemned earlier that month from Bromsgrove shed and broken up at Derby Works. Its headlight had been transferred to BR Standard 2-10-0 Class '9F' No. 92079. *(M.E. Kirk/Martyn Reeve Collection)*

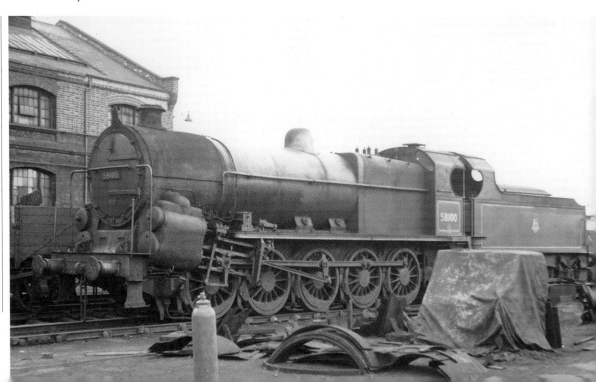

Fowler Compound 4-4-0 No. 40930 on Derby shed awaiting its next duty on 12 May 1956. Built in 1927 at the Vulcan Foundry, it was withdrawn in April 1957 from Gloucester shed and disposed of here at the Works. *(M.E. Kirk/Martyn Reeve Collection)*

Johnson 0-6-0 Class '2F' No. 58247 is ready to go back into traffic in May 1956 after a visit to the adjacent Works. Built in 1887 at Derby Works, it was scrapped there when withdrawn from Rowsley shed in January 1958. *(M.E. Kirk/Martyn Reeve Collection)*

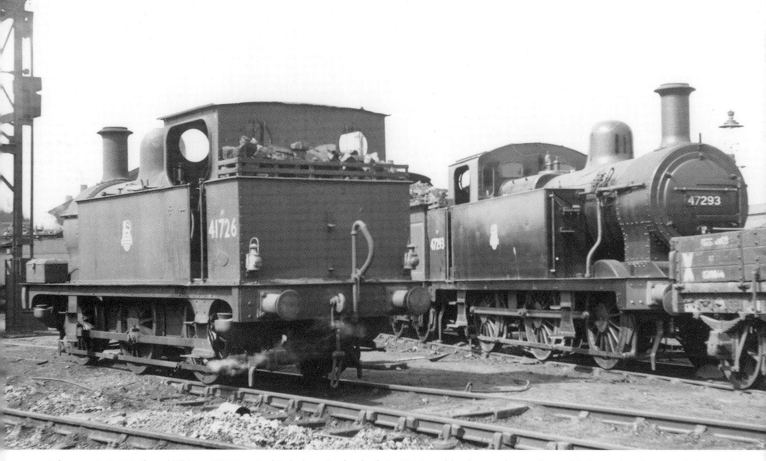

Johnson 0-6-0T Class '1F' No. 41726 at its birthplace Derby, built in 1883 and broken up here when withdrawn in July 1959 from Derby shed. To the right is Fowler 0-6-0T Class '3F' No. 47293, fresh off the Works. Manufactured in 1924 by the North British Locomotive Co. Glasgow and condemned in December 1966, it was cut up by J. McWilliams, Shettleston. *(M.E. Kirk/Martyn Reeve Collection)*

Johnson 0-6-0 Class '2F' No. 58293, pictured here on 12 May 1956 after having received a light casual in the Works. Built by Kitson in 1897, it was condemned in January 1961 from Barrow shed and broken up at Central Wagon Co., Wigan. *(M.E. Kirk/Martyn Reeve Collection)*

Johnson 0-6-0T Class '1F' No. 41726 at its birthplace, built in 1883 and broken up here when withdrawn in July 1959 from Derby shed. *(M.E. Kirk/Martyn Reeve Collection)*

Minus its tender, Compound 4-4-0 No. 41192 is receiving attention on 12 May 1956. Built in 1927 at the Vulcan Foundry, it has only another year in service before withdrawal from Derby Shed and cutting-up at the nearby Works. *(M.E. Kirk/Martyn Reeve Collection)*

Johnson 0-6-0T Class '1F' No. 41805, built in 1891 at Derby Works and disposed of there was condemned from Canklow shed in April 1956, a month before this picture was taken. *(M.E. Kirk/Martyn Reeve Collection)*

Photographed on 19 April 1957, Johnson 0-6-0 Class '3F' No. 43658, built in 1900 at the Vulcan Foundry and condemned in September 1963 from Derby shed shown here with No. 43368, built in 1891 by Dubs & Co. and withdrawn in November 1961 from Derby shed. Both were cut-up at Derby Works. *(M.E. Kirk/Martyn Reeve Collection)*

CHAPTER 3

DERBY FRIARGATE/ GN ENVIRONS

Gresley 2-6-0 Class 'K2' No. 61749 arrives at Derby Friargate station on 10 July 1954 with the 2pm express from Mablethorpe. Built in 1916 at Doncaster Works and withdrawn from Colwick shed in January 1959, it was scrapped at Darlington Works. *(M.E. Kirk/Martyn Reeve Collection)*

The 12.55pm (SO) Llandudno to Nottingham (Victoria) express is entering Friargate station on 10 July 1954 hauled by Thompson 4-6-0 Class 'B1' No. 61209. Manufactured by the North British Locomotive Company Glasgow in 1947 and withdrawn after a relatively short life from Colwick shed in September 1962, it was disposed of by Albert Loom, Spondon. A 0-6-2T Class 'N1' is on the right. *(M.E. Kirk/Martyn Reeve Collection)*

Latter days of the Nottingham (Victoria) to Derby (Friargate) service which was withdrawn on 5 September 1964. Here at Friargate on 23 July 1964, Ivatt 2-6-0 Class '4MT' No. 43145 has arrived with 6.25pm stopping train from Nottingham Victoria. Built in 1951 at Doncaster Works, it was withdrawn in January 1965 from Colwick shed and scrapped by T.W. Ward, Beighton. *(Tony Smith)*

The Saturday only Kings Norton-Skegness express hauled by a Stanier 'Black Five' leaving Mickleover tunnel in September 1963. This was the penultimate year of operation over this route. *(Tony Smith)*

An unidentified 'Jubilee' 4-6-0 Class '6P' passing Mickleover in August 1964 during the last year of operation of the Kings Norton to Skegness train via the GN route. This train was the last booked passenger train between Eggington Junction and Derby Friargate and ran on Summer Saturdays with a corresponding return service. In 1965, the train was diverted to run via Derby Midland, Nottingham Midland and Netherfield Junction. *(Tony Smith)*

CHAPTER 4

EASTBOUND TO TRENT VIA MIDLAND MAIN LINE

The Midland was a railway of distinction. Its signal boxes were of wooden construction, the lower half up to floor level finished in overlapping horizontal boarding, painted in banana yellow with plum ends and surrounds. The large window frames were white, some opening whilst others were fixed. Identification of the signal box was by means of a name board at either end. Sheet Stores Junction signal box, where I worked, was of standard Midland Railway design. This view is looking southeast where LMS 2-8-0 '8F' No. 48646 is working a Beeston-Chaddesden freight on 15 July 1964 on the south curve from Trent station. It was built in 1943 at Brighton Works and condemned from Lostock Hall shed in December 1968. The line to the right is from Leicester. *(Roderick H. Fowkes)*

Not the best of photographs but the awesome power of this magnificent, majestic Beyer-Garratt 2-6-6-2T No. 47991 is evident in all its splendour captured here with steam to spare after negotiating the final 1-in-220 rising gradient to Sheet Stores Junction. However, perhaps all is not well; the driver is looking back and that could be the fireman walking alongside the train which has just run onto the Castle Donington branch with a Toton-Washwood Heath mineral train in this undated picture. Built in 1930 by Beyer-Peacock, No. 47991 was condemned from Toton shed in December 1955 and disposed of at Crewe Works. (*Photograph courtesy of the late Claude Cook*)

One of the highlights of the day in and around Trent was the sight of named trains, such as 'The Thames-Clyde Express' and 'The Palatine'. Pictured here, in May 1956, the train engine, 'Jubilee' 4-6-0 No. 45615 *Malay States* is carrying the headboard of 'The Thames-Clyde Express', 9.20am Glasgow (St Enoch) to London (St Pancras) and has steam to spare, now getting into its stride after leaving Trent station in May 1956 piloted by Johnson 4-4-0 Class '2P' No. 40542. The 'Jubilee' was built in 1934 at Crewe Works and cut up there when withdrawn from Burton shed in December 1962, and 40542 emerged in 1899 from Derby Works and was withdrawn from Nottingham shed with just short of sixty years service and broken up at T.W. Ward, Killamarsh. (*Joe Wade*)

Considering its importance as a major junction, Trent station presented a sometimes totally deserted picture; though for most of the time the platforms were bare of passengers, the volume of traffic passing through made it a delight for enthusiasts. Here, a view of the island station with its canopies over the platforms from the Trent North Junction signal box as the 8.07am Derby to Nottingham stopping train departs on 3 July 1956. In charge of the train is Post-Grouping development of Johnson Midland compound design, Fowler 3-cylinder 4-4-0 Class '4P' No. 41095, leaking like a sieve. It was built in 1925 at Derby Works and disposed of there when withdrawn in February 1958 from Gloucester shed. (*Tony Smith*)

Passing Trent Station North Junction signalbox and entering the station is Fowler 2-6-4T Class '4P' No. 42330 with a Nottingham to Leicester stopping train in July 1955. Built in 1929 at Derby Works, it was scrapped there when condemned in December 1961 from Leicester shed. (*Joe Wade*)

Infiltration by ex-GCR 'D11' or 'Director' Class 4-4-0s allocated to the Eastern Region depot at Lincoln became commonplace on the former Midland lines in the mid-1950s. On 9 July 1956, the 3.05pm Lincoln to Derby express leaves Trent station hauled by No. 62666 *Zeebrugge*. The 'D11s' were later to be replaced by ex-GER 'Claud Hamilton' or 'D16/3' Class 4-4-0s in 1957, before they too were succeeded a year later by lightweight diesel-multiple-units. Built in 1922 at Gorton Works, *Zeebrugge* was withdrawn in December 1960 from Sheffield (Darnall) shed and cut up at Doncaster Works. (*Tony Smith*)

Clearly showing the rural aspect around Trent station, and with just 119¾ miles left to run to London, 'The Thames-Clyde Express' eases out of the platform on 1 June 1956 on its way headed by Kentish Town 'Jubilee' 4-6-0 Class '6P' No. 45612 *Jamaica* that has worked through from Leeds City. Built in 1934 at Crewe Works, it was broken up there when withdrawn in March 1964 from Derby shed. (*Tony Smith*)

Despite having a stud of eighteen 'Jubilees' on its books, Leeds (Holbeck) shed was no doubt short of power on this day in June 1959 as Stanier 4-6-0 'Black Five' No. 44849 deputises for the rostered 'Jubilee' on 'The Thames-Clyde Express' coasting towards its Trent stop. In view of this, a pilot engine would probably be attached at Leicester in order to maintain time. Built in 1944 at Crewe Works, No. 44849 was scrapped there when withdrawn in December 1965 from Leeds (Holbeck) shed. (*Joe Wade*)

Liverpool (Edge Hill)-allocated Fowler 'Patriot' non-rebuilt Class 4-6-0 No. 45518 *Bradshaw* recently ex-Works from Crewe on what would turn out to be its last Heavy Intermediate repair, awaits the road off the goods line at Long Eaton Junction with an Edge Hill to Nottingham freight in 1961. Within three months of this photograph being taken *Bradshaw* would be transferred away to Lancaster, where it would end its working days upon its withdrawal at the end of October 1962 before being disposed of at Horwich Works. (*Joe Wade*)

CHAPTER 5

EREWASH VALLEY LINE - TOTON

All ten of the Franco-Crosti boilered 2-10-0 '9Fs' were initially allocated to Wellingborough shed from new. Seen here in original form, exhausting steam through its side chimney, No. 92024 is on the goods line near Trent working a Toton-Brent mineral train in June 1957. The engine is blowing off and the open cylinder cocks, together with the white exhaust, suggest that it might have 'picked up the water'. This was another locomotive which suffered the ignominy of being condemned, again from Birkenhead shed with less than thirteen years service to be disposed of at Campbells, Airdrie. (*Joe Wade*)

Stanier 2-8-0 Class '8F' No. 48271 left Toton West Yard a few minutes earlier negotiating the two level crossings at Long Eaton station and North Erewash Junction and is now in full cry blasting away laying a trail of black smoke as it rattles over Trent Station North Junction with a Toton-Birmingham (Washwood Heath) mineral train on 3 May 1959. It was manufactured in 1942 by North British Locomotive Company, Glasgow and condemned from Northwich shed in August 1967. (*Tony Smith*)

Beyer-Garratt Class 2-6-6-2T No. 47969, with its distinctive revolving bunker, runs bunker-first with a Clay Cross to Wellingborough train of empty iron-ore tippler and hopper wagons for the Northamptonshire ore fields as it passes Meadow Lane Junction on the High Level goods line in May 1957. Toton driver William (Bill) Webb revered these locomotives and liked nothing better than running bunker first, where he could sit with his feet up without smoke and steam enveloping the cab and obscuring the sighting of signals. No. 47969 was withdrawn from Hasland shed in August 1957 and disposed of at Crewe Works. (*Joe Wade*)

On its way home, Northampton-allocated Stanier LMS 2-8-0 Class '8F' No. 48305 crosses the viaduct over the River Trent on the Up goods line with a southbound freight from Toton Yard in June 1957. Built in 1943 at Crewe Works and withdrawn in 1968 from Speke Junction shed, fortunately the locomotive was rescued from Woodham's scrapyard in South Wales, the lifeline that saw it returned to steam at Loughborough on the preserved Great Central Railway. (*Joe Wade*)

Midland 0-6-0 Class '4F' No. 44131 emerges from Red Hill New Tunnel in September 1960 with a southbound freight from Toton Yard. Built in 1925 at Crewe Works, it was withdrawn in November 1964 from Bury Shed and broken up by T.W. Ward, Killamarsh in 1965. (*Joe Wade*)

Johnson Midland design, rebuilt by Fowler from 1916 with non superheated Belpaire boiler is 0-6-0 Class '3F' No. 43751 a few miles south of Trent, unusually on the main line in Sutton Bonington cutting between Kegworth and Hathern in April 1958 working an up southbound mineral train. This 1901 build by Neilson & Co. was withdrawn from Sheffield (Grimesthorpe) shed in August 1961 and scrapped at Crewe Works. (*Joe Wade*)

The 11.45am London (St Pancras)-Bradford (Forster Square) express now well into its stride at Long Eaton after the Trent station stop is headed by Jubilee 4-6-0 Class '6P' 45573 *Newfoundland* on 29 June 1954, manufactured by the North British Locomotive Company, Glasgow in 1934, withdrawn from Leeds (Holbeck) shed in August 1965 and scrapped at Clayton & Davie, Dunston-on-Tyne. The leading van is a GNR bogie milk van of 1909 vintage. (*M.E. Kirk/Martyn Reeve Collection*)

Driver William (Bill) Webb on the footplate of British Railways Standard 4-6-0 Class '5MT' No. 73031 at Toton Motive Power Depot in late 1953. Both 73030 and 73031, new from Derby Works in July 1953 were fitted with air brake gear in connection with a series of Westinghouse Brake Trials conducted between Trowell Junction and Ilkeston South Junction on the Erewash Valley line and also Special Test trains between Toton and Bedford. *(Roderick H. Fowkes)*

Fowler/Beyer-Peacock 2-6-6-2T Beyer-Garratt No. 47973 at Toton Motive Power Depot on 13 May 1956. Built in 1930 by Beyer Peacock Ltd., and withdrawn in April 1957 from Hasland shed, it was scrapped at Crewe Works. Some fastidious drivers objected to running bunker first and the Toton Local Departmental Committee in 1931 submitted a complaint on behalf of men working the Garratt engines tender first, which was declined by the Company's representatives. *(M.E. Kirk/Martyn Reeve Collection)*

Photographed on the Garratt Road at Toton shed on 13 May 1956. Before the introduction of those giant 2-6-6-2T locomotives, the Toton-Brent coal trains were double-headed by Class '3F' and '4F' 0-6-0 tender engines. Here at rest are 47981, 47998, 47996, which were condemned from Toton during 1956 and 47994 withdrawn from Hasland shed in March 1958; all were cut up at Crewe Works. *(M.E. Kirk/Martyn Reeve Collection)*

BR Standard 4-6-0 Class '5MT' No. 73031, fitted with Westinghouse equipment on number 2 down goods line at Ilkeston South Junction in late 1953, during a series of trials with continuous brakes on mineral trains which took place on the Midland main line. Built at Derby Works in June of that year and withdrawn in September 1965 from Oxford shed and broken up at Cashmore's, Newport. *(Roderick H. Fowkes)*

A northbound freight train at Pye Bridge on 5 July 1954 is hauled by Fowler 0-6-0 Class '4F' No. 43982, built in 1922 by Armstrong Whitworth and withdrawn from Kirkby-in-Ashfield shed in June 1965, disposed of at Cashmore's, Great Bridge. Midland 0-6-0 Class '3F' No. 43580, alongside, was built by Kitson, withdrawn in April 1961 from Trafford Park shed and scrapped at Central Wagon Co. Wigan. *(M.E. Kirk/Martyn Reeve Collection)*

S.L.S SPECIAL, Derbyshire & Notts. Rail Tour seen here at Ripley on 21 April 1956 hauled by BR Standard 2-6-2T Class '2MT' 84008, which was built in 1953 at Crewe Works and withdrawn after only twelve years service from Leicester shed and scrapped at Buttigiegs, Newport. *(M.E. Kirk/Martyn Reeve Collection)*

CHAPTER 6

BEESTON

A train of empty stock hurries through Beeston station on 2 April 1956 with Midland 4-4-0 Class '2P' 40411 in charge. Built in 1892 by Sharp, Stewart and Company, it was withdrawn in February 1961 from Nottingham shed and cut up by Albert Loom, Spondon. *(M.E. Kirk/Martyn Reeve Collection)*

A 1956 Easter Monday excursion, the 11.10am Nottingham-Belle Vue arriving at Beeston with Mogul 2-6-0 Class '6P5F' No. 42769. This was built in 1927 at Crewe Works and withdrawn from Gorton shed in February 1964 and broken up at Hesslewoods, Attercliffe. These locomotives were ideal for excursion and holiday traffic when not used for freight work. The first coach is an LNWR 3rd corridor M2668M. *(M.E. Kirk/Martyn Reeve Collection)*

CHAPTER 7

NOTTINGHAM MIDLAND STATION

Long term Nottingham 16A-allocated 'Jubilee' 4-6-0 Class '6P' 45636 *Uganda* is on its way from Nottingham MPD to the station for a special duty on 13 May 1956. Built in 1934 at Crewe Works and withdrawn in December 1962 from Burton shed, it was later cut up at Crewe Works. *(M.E. Kirk/Martyn Reeve Collection)*

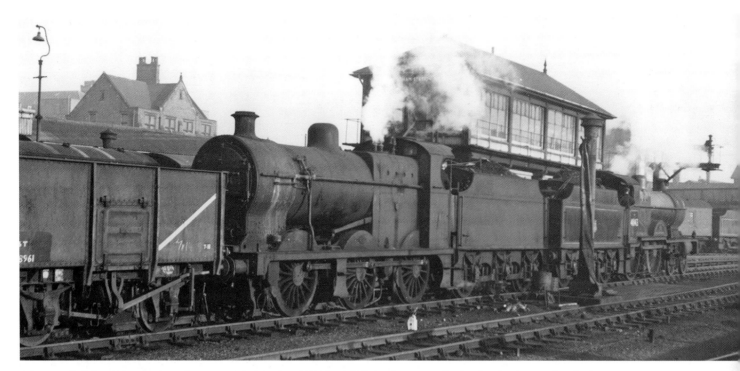

A brace of Midland locomotives, Compound 4-4-0 Class '4P' No. 41143 has been attached to Fowler 0-6-0 Class '4F' No. 44408 on an eastbound freight train passing through Nottingham Midland station on 24 December 1954. No. 41143, a product from the NBL Co. Glasgow in 1925, was withdrawn in March 1959 from Derby shed and scrapped at Crewe Works. The '4F' was built in 1927 at Derby Works, condemned from Normanton shed in October 1965 and cut up at Garnham, Harris & Elton, Chesterfield. *(M.E. Kirk/Martyn Reeve Collection)*

Seen here at Nottingham Midland station on 4 March 1955, a pair of work stained locomotives; a Fowler rebuild of Johnson design Class '2P' 40454 is acting as station pilot and leaving the platform is Robinson-designed 4-4-0 ex-GCR No. 62660 *Butler-Henderson,* with the 11.22am stopping service to Lincoln (St Marks). Quite unexpectedly in the mid-1950s, five Robinson-designed ex-GCR 'D11' or 'Director' Class' 4-4-0s allocated to the Easter Region depot at Lincoln began to permeate the former Midland lines. *(M.E. Kirk/Martyn Reeve Collection)*

The day after the previous photograph was taken, 4-4-0 Class '2P' No. 40454 is having a main line run out heading the 4.20pm stopping train to Kings Lynn via Melton Mowbray and Spalding. Built in 1894 at Derby Works, it was condemned from Nottingham shed in September 1960 and broken up at Gorton Works. *(M.E. Kirk/Martyn Reeve Collection)*

Also on this day, 'D11/1' 62660 *Butler-Henderson* was again present as regular haulage by an Eastern Region locomotive on the 3.05pm Lincoln (St Marks)-Derby (Midland) semi-fast, one of five locomotives allocated to the Eastern Region depot at Lincoln (40A) in the mid-1950s. *(M.E. Kirk/Martyn Reeve Collection)*

A closer look at the deplorable external condition of Robinson Class 4-4-0 'D11' No. 62660 Butler-Henderson with a Lincoln-Derby express standing underneath the Great Central line overbridge. Following its withdrawal in November 1960 from Sheffield (Darnall) shed, No. 62660 would be preserved by the British Transport Commission and restored to full Great Central livery. *(M.E. Kirk/Martyn Reeve Collection)*

Johnson-designed 4-4-0 Class '2P' No. 40458 is bringing in the coaches for the 11.38am stopping train to Worksop from the carriage sidings on 18 June 1955. It was built in 1894 at Derby Works and scrapped there when withdrawn from Nottingham shed in February 1957. *(M.E. Kirk/Martyn Reeve Collection)*

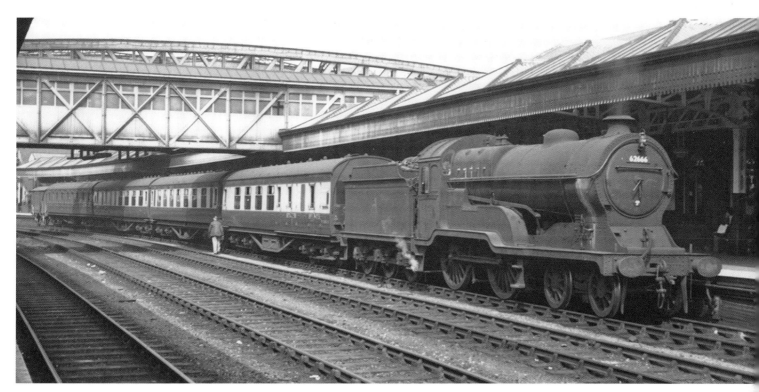

The former Midland shed at Lincoln had come under the control of the Eastern Region and although a small number of L.M. engines were still serviced there, most of the through workings between Lincoln and Derby were in the hands of Eastern Region locomotives. The 9.10am local stopping train from Derby has arrived at Nottingham station on 21 July 1955 behind Robinson 4-4-0 'D11' No. 62666 *Zeebrugge*, built in 1922 at Gorton Works, withdrawn from Sheffield (Darnall) shed in December 1960 and disposed of at Doncaster Works. *(M.E. Kirk/Martyn Reeve Collection)*

An 11.14am Nottingham to St Pancras relief train is composed of Midland suburban stock and hauled by Fowler Compound No. 41144 on 6 August 1955. Built in 1925 at the NBL Co. Glasgow and withdrawn in March 1958 from Bournville shed, it was disposed of at Derby Works. On the left is Fowler 0-6-0 No. 43874 having arrived with the 10.20am (SO) local from Mansfield. This was built in 1918 at Derby Works and cut up there when withdrawn from Mansfield shed in March 1956. *(M.E. Kirk/Martyn Reeve Collection)*

Arriving at Nottingham station on 10 March 1956 with the 2.35pm stopping train from Leicester is Fowler 2-6-4T Class '4P' No. 42342, built in 1929 at Derby Works and disposed of there when withdrawn from Kentish Town shed in June 1962. *(M.E. Kirk/ Martyn Reeve Collection)*

Although displaying express headlights, the 10am Easter Monday special M702, Nottingham to Buxton (Midland) train in April 1956 will be calling at all stations via Long Eaton and Butterley, hauled by Fowler 0-6-0 '4F' No. 44555. Built in 1928 at Crewe Works and withdrawn from Nottingham shed in March 1960, it was scrapped by T.W. Ward, Killamarsh. *(M.E. Kirk/Martyn Reeve Collection)*

A filthy Robinson 4-4-0 Class D11/1 62667 *Somme* has picked up a LNWR corridor Brake van M32104 to attach to the 11.23am local train from Nottingham to Lincoln (St Marks) on 14 April 1956. Built in 1922 at Gorton Works, it was withdrawn in August 1960 from Sheffield (Darnall) shed and broken up at Doncaster Works. *(M.E. Kirk/Martyn Reeve Collection)*

The 9.20am Lincoln-Derby semi-fast is arriving on Whit Monday in 1956 behind Compound 4-4-0 No. 41143, built in 1925 by the North British Locomotive Co. Glasgow and condemned in March 1959 from Derby shed and disposed of at Crewe Works. The leading coach is M19597. *(M.E. Kirk/Martyn Reeve Collection)*

A pair of Fowler 0-6-0s awaits the arrival of M956 excursion train at Nottingham Midland station on Whit Monday in May 1956. Class '4F' No.43954, built in 1921 by Armstrong Whitworth and No. 43917, built in 1920 at Derby Works, both withdrawn in 1964 and scrapped at T.W. Ward, Killamarsh. *(M.E. Kirk/Martyn Reeve Collection)*

Another Whit Monday excursion train from Nottingham, Fowler 0-6-0 Class '4F' No. 44215 is ready to depart with the **10.05am** to Buxton via Butterley. Built at Derby Works in 1925, it was withdrawn from Kirkby-in-Ashfield shed in February 1965 and cut up at T.W. Ward, Killamarsh. Tender first on the right is another Fowler 0-6-0 No. 44030. *(M.E. Kirk/Martyn Reeve Collection)*

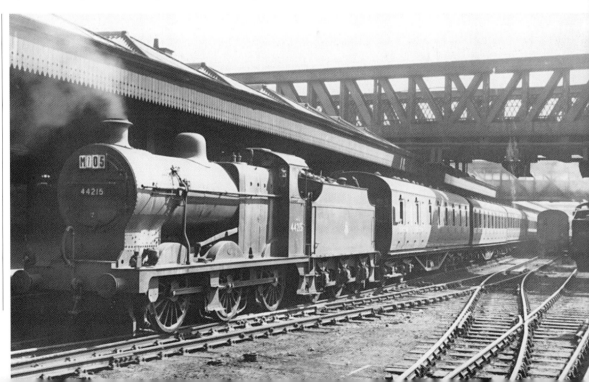

Lincoln (40A) Motive Power Depot must have been short of engine cleaners judging by the condition of Robinson 4-4-0 Class 'D11/1' No. 62670 *Marne*, bound for Lincoln (St Marks) on 29 September 1956 with a local stopping train. Built in 1922 at Gorton Works and withdrawn in November 1960 from Sheffield (Darnall) shed, it was broken up at Doncaster Works. *(M.E. Kirk/Martyn Reeve Collection)*

Super power for the 9.20am semi-fast Lincoln-Derby express on 24 August 1957, with Fowler 0-6-0 Class '4F' No. 43856 piloting Ivatt 2-6-0 Class '4MT' No. 43040. The 0-6-0 was built in 1918 at Derby Works and condemned in September 1964. The 'Flying Pig' was built in 1949 at Horwich Works and withdrawn in November 1966 and broken up by Clayton & Davie, Dunston-on-Tyne. *(M.E. Kirk/Martyn Reeve Collection)*

The 7.20am Bradford (Forster Square)-London (St Pancras) is arriving behind Nottingham-allocated 'Jubilee' 4-6-0 Class '6P' No. 45667 *Jellicoe* in August 1957. Built in 1935 at Crewe Works, *Jellicoe* was withdrawn from Bank Hall shed in January 1965 and cut up by Maden & McKee, Liverpool. *(M.E. Kirk/Martyn Reeve Collection)*

Now taking on water at Nottingham station in August 1957, the next opportunity being the water troughs at Brentingby near Melton Mowbray, we see 'Jubilee' 4-6-0 Class '6P' No. 45667 *Jellicoe* with the 7.20am express from Bradford (Forster Square) to London (St Pancras). *(M.E. Kirk/Martyn Reeve Collection)*

With a rake of twelve coaches, Fowler 2-6-4T Class '4P' No. 42400 and Fowler 0-6-0 Class '4F' 44420 head the 9.55am (SO) Derby to Yarmouth (Beach)-Cromer (Beach)-Lowestoft (Central) & Gorleston-on-Sea express arriving in Nottingham station on 24 August 1957. Both locomotives were built at Derby Works in 1933 and 1927 respectively, No. 42400 was withdrawn from Stafford shed in January 1965 and No. 44420 condemned in September of the same year from Westhouses shed and both were cut up at Cashmore's, Great Bridge. *(M.E. Kirk/Martyn Reeve Collection)*

Now seen leaving Nottingham station is the 9.55am (SO) Derby-Yarmouth (Beach)-Cromer(Beach)-Lowestoft(Central) & Gorleston-on Sea express headed by Fowler 2-6-4T Class '4MT' No. 42400 piloting Fowler 0-6-0 Class '4F' 44420. The pilot engine will be detached at Saxby as will the Lowestoft & Gorleston-on-Sea portion which will go forward on the 10.52am service from Leicester. *(M.E. Kirk/Martyn Reeve Collection)*

On 12 August 1961, Stanier 'Jubilee' 4-6-0 Class '6P' No. 45667 *Jellicoe* is running tender first to the carriage sidings to bring the empty stock into the station to work a relief train to the 'Waverley' express for Edinburgh. Built in 1935 at Crewe Works and withdrawn in January 1965 from Bank Hall shed, it was disposed of at Maden & McKee, Liverpool. *(M.E. Kirk/Martyn Reeve Collection)*

'Jubilee' 4-6-0 Class '6P' No. 45667 *Jellicoe* is entering the platform having collected the coaches from the carriage sidings for the 11.20am Nottingham to Edinburgh train, a relief to the 'Waverley'. The reporting number for the express has now been changed from 1S50 to 1X55. *(M.E. Kirk/Martyn Reeve Collection)*

Off the beaten track, with 1M33 chalked on the smokebox door, Newton Heath-allocated 'Jubilee' 4-6-0 Class '6P' No. 45700 *Amethyst* arrives at Nottingham station with a relief train on 9 September 1961. Built in 1936 at Crewe Works, it was scrapped there when withdrawn from Warrington (Dallam) shed in July 1964. *(M.E. Kirk/Martyn Reeve Collection)*

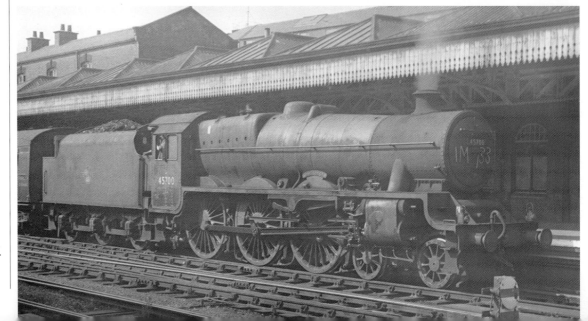

CHAPTER 8

NOTTINGHAM VICTORIA STATION

The 1.12pm (SO) stopping train from Pinxton has arrived in Nottingham Victoria station on 19 January 1952 behind Ivatt 0-6-0 Class 'J1' No. 65008. Built in 1908 at Doncaster Works, it was scrapped there when withdrawn from Colwick shed two months after this picture was taken. *(M.E. Kirk/Martyn Reeve Collection)*

Robinson 4-6-2T Class 'A5' No. 69807 has just arrived at Nottingham Victoria station on 16 August 1952, working the 10.40am (SO) service from Edwinstowe via Mansfield (Central). Built in 1911 at Gorton Works and condemned in July 1958 from Colwick shed, it was broken up at Darlington Works. *(M.E. Kirk/Martyn Reeve Collection)*

A busy evening scene at Nottingham Victoria station on 23 August 1952. Left to Right, Gresley 2-6-0 Class 'K3' 61976, built in 1936 at Darlington Works, withdrawn from Sheffield (Darnall) shed in January 1962 and cut up at Doncaster Works. Ivatt 0-6-0 'J5' No. 65487 with the 6.05pm to Basford & Bulwell via Gedling was built in 1910 at Doncaster Works and had less than a year before withdrawal from Colwick shed in June 1953. Ivatt/Gresley 0-6-0 'J6' No. 64237 waits with the 6.15pm to Grantham. This was built in 1914 at Doncaster Works and scrapped there when withdrawn in November 1959 from Hitchin shed. Johnson 4-4-0 Class '2P' No. 40534 has a while to wait before it leaves with the 6.34pm to Northampton (Castle). Built in 1899 at Derby Works, it was withdrawn from Nottingham shed in July 1959 and disposed of by T.W. Ward, Killamarsh. *(M.E. Kirk/Martyn Reeve Collection)*

Gresley 4-6-2 Class 'A3' 60048 *Doncaster* is at rest at Nottingham Victoria in August 1953 after arriving with a local service. Built in 1934 at Doncaster Works and withdrawn from Grantham shed in September 1963, it was rather poignantly cut up at its birthplace. *(M.E. Kirk/Martyn Reeve Collection)*

An early afternoon scene at Nottingham Victoria station in June 1954, with Thompson 'B1' No. 61269 in the middle road with empty stock. Built in 1947 at the NBL Co. Glasgow, it was withdrawn from Gorton shed after just fifteen years service and cut up at T.W. Ward, Killamarsh. Ivatt/Gresley 0-6-0 Class 'J6' No. 64273 is working the 2.05pm local train to Derby (Friargate); this was built in 1922 at Doncaster Works and broken up there when withdrawn from Colwick shed in December 1959. *(M.E. Kirk/Martyn Reeve Collection)*

Station pilot, Ivatt 0-6-2T Class 'N1' No. 69481, shunting empty compartment stock at Nottingham Victoria station in June 1954, the leading coach of which is of North Eastern Railway origin. The locomotive was built in 1912 at Doncaster Works and broken up there when withdrawn from Ardsley shed in May 1956. *(M.E. Kirk/Martyn Reeve Collection)*

Standing at platform 1 adding to the smoke haze is Ivatt 0-6-2T Class 'N1' No. 69476 waiting to depart with the 9.18am (SO) Nottingham (Victoria)-Mansfield (Central)-Edwinstowe stopping train on 26 June 1954. Built in 1912 at Doncaster Works, it was disposed of there when condemned from Colwick shed in March 1955. *(M.E. Kirk/Martyn Reeve Collection)*

The north end of Nottingham Victoria station was dominated by the stark plate girder road bridge across eight platforms and fourteen tracks, although the lofty clock tower imparted some dignity over the whole scene. In Bay platform 3 on Saturday 10 July 1954, the 3.40pm Saturdays-only service to Shirebrook North is ready to leave behind Gresley 0-6-0 Class 'J39' No. 64832. Built in 1932 at Doncaster Works and condemned from Colwick shed in September 1959, it was cut up at Stratford Works. Alongside is Ivatt 0-6-0 Class 'J5' No. 65498, with the 4.08pm for Pinxton. No. 65498 was built in 1909 at Doncaster Works and disposed of there when withdrawn from Colwick shed at the end of 1955. *(M.E. Kirk/Martyn Reeve Collection)*

Robinson 4-6-2T Class 'A5' No. 69809 is steam heating empty coaching stock including a pair of Gresley twins in the centre road Nottingham Victoria station on 4 March 1955. Built in 1912 at Gorton Works, this locomotive was condemned from Colwick shed in May 1959 and broken up at Darlington Works. *(M.E. Kirk/Martyn Reeve Collection)*

On Saturday 16 July 1955, bright sunshine streams through the train shed roof as the 10.15am Bradford (Exchange)-Poole express arrives at Nottingham Victoria at platform 7 headed by Stanier 'Black Five' No. 44912, built in 1945 at Crewe Works and withdrawn in September 1967 from Leeds (Holbeck) shed and disposed of at Cashmore's, Great Bridge. *(M.E. Kirk/Martyn Reeve Collection)*

A busy lunchtime scene at Nottingham Victoria station in late July 1955. Thompson 4-6-0 'B1' No. 61056 stands in the through road, manufactured in 1946 by the NBL Co. Glasgow, withdrawn from Immingham shed in April 1964 and scrapped at Central Wagon Co. Wigan. Gresley 4-6-2 'A3' No. 60102 *Sir Frederick Banbury* is hauling the 10am Bradford (Exchange) to London (Marylebone), 'The South Yorkshireman', built in 1922 at Doncaster Works and cut up there when withdrawn from Kings Cross shed in November 1961. Ivatt/Gresley 0-6-0 Class 'J6' No. 64273, was built in 1922 at Doncaster Works and broken up there when condemned in December 1959 from Colwick shed. Gresley 2-6-0 Class 'K2' No. 61738, was built in 1914 at Doncaster Works, withdrawn from Colwick shed in July 1959 and disposed of at Darlington Works. *(M.E. Kirk/Martyn Reeve Collection)*

Thompson 4-6-0 'B1' No. 61390 is waiting for the road at Nottingham Victoria station on 30 July 1955 with a seaside extra to the east coast. Built in 1951 by the NBL Co. Glasgow and withdrawn from Colwick shed in February 1966, it was cut up at Birds, Long Marston. The formation includes GER Corridor 3rd E61419E & GCR Corridor 3rd E5270E. *(M.E. Kirk/ Martyn Reeve Collection)*

A line up of Thompson locos under a dreary spring sky on Saturday 14 April 1956. 'B1' No. 61106 waits to leave platform 4 with the 12.10pm football excursion to Wadsley Bridge. This locomotive was built in 1946 by NBL Co. Glasgow and withdrawn in November 1962 from Woodford Halse shed before being broken up at Darlington Works. In Bay platform 3, the 1.15pm local to Sutton-in-Ashfield (Town) has 'L1' No. 67760, another North British product of 1948, condemned in August 1961 from Colwick shed and cut up at Darlington Works. On the right is 'L1' No. 67799 in charge of the 12.15pm to Pinxton South. Built in 1950 by Robert Stephenson & Hawthorn Ltd., it was withdrawn from Colwick shed in March 1962 and scrapped at Darlington Works. *(M.E. Kirk/Martyn Reeve Collection)*

Holiday traffic to the east coast resorts often merited a relief train, as was the case on Whit Monday 1956 at Nottingham Victoria as the 10.50am New Basford-Skegness arrives behind Gresley 2-6-0 Class 'K2' No. 61748. Built in 1916 at Doncaster Works and withdrawn from Boston shed in June 1959, it was disposed of at Motherwell Machinery & Scrap, Wishaw. The leading coach is E5659E. *(M.E. Kirk/Martyn Reeve Collection)*

Thompson 4-6-0 Class 'B1' No. 61160 is ready to leave the station with the 4.30pm to Skegness on Good Friday 1957. Built in 1947 at the Vulcan Foundry, it was withdrawn in September 1963 from Colwick shed at and scrapped at Cashmore's Great Bridge. *(M.E. Kirk/Martyn Reeve Collection)*

Ivatt 2-6-0 Class '4MT' No. 43064 is seen here at Nottingham Victoria on 16 May 1963 having effected enginemen's relief. Built in 1950 at Doncaster Works and withdrawn from Langwith Junction shed in June 1965, No. 43064 was cut up at T.W.Ward, Beighton. *(Tony Smith)*

Annesley Shed had inherited a variety of 'Royal Scot' and 'Britannia' Class '7P' locomotives, most in a poor mechanical condition. Here, BR Standard 'Britannia' Pacific No. 70050 *Firth of Clyde* provides the motive power for the 5.15pm Nottingham Victoria-Marylebone semi-fast on 16 May 1963. Built in 1954 at Crewe Works and withdrawn in August 1966 from Carlisle (Kingmoor) Shed, it was scrapped at Campbells, Airdrie. *(Tony Smith)*

Latter days on the Great Central. The Ramsgate to Derby (Friargate) train pulls out of Loughborough (Central) station on 8 August 1964 headed by Stanier 'Black Five' No. 45346. Manufactured in 1937 by Armstrong Whitworth and withdrawn from Stockport (Edgeley) shed in June 1967 and cut up at Cashmore's, Great Bridge. This is the return working of the 11.35pm (Fridays Only) from Derby Friargate and was the last year the South Coast holiday trains were run over the GC route with the sole exception of the York-Bournemouth all the year round service. The Ramsgate service was, in 1965 diverted via Brent and the Midland main line to terminate at Nottingham Midland. (*Tony Smith*)

Pictured at Leicester Central station on 6 June 1963 is BR Standard 4-6-0 Class '5' No. 73159 working a Grimsby-Swindon Fish train. It was built in 1957 at Doncaster Works and withdrawn from Patricroft shed in October 1967 before being scrapped at Cashmore's, Newport. (*Tony Smith*)

Activity at Leicester Central station on 6 June 1963 with Stanier 4-6-0 'Black Five' No. 45334 working the 5.15pm Nottingham Victoria-London Marylebone semi-fast express. Built in 1937 by Armstrong Whitworth and condemned from Annesley shed in July 1965, it was finally broken up at Cashmore's, Great Bridge. *(Tony Smith)*

The London extension of the Great Central Railway sees Annesley-allocated Royal Scot 4-6-0 Class '7P' No. 46101 *Royal Scots Grey* languishing in the siding outside Marylebone station devoid of steam. A NBL product of 1927 and condemned in September 1963, it was moved to store at Willesden shed before being cut up at Slag Reduction Co. Ltd, Ickles, Rotherham in April 1964. I travelled on the 8.15am Nottingham Victoria-Marylebone on 1 July 1963 when 46101 had to be removed at Leicester Central short of steam. In front is Stanier Class '5' No. 45234 after working 8.15am from Nottingham Victoria on 12 August 1963. *(Roderick H. Fowkes)*

CHAPTER 9

ENVIRONS OF NOTTINGHAM AND BEYOND

Arriving at Awsworth station on 29 June 1954 is the 12.45pm Nottingham (Victoria)-Derby (Friargate) local train hauled by Ivatt 0-6-2T Class 'N1' No. 69451, built in 1910 at Doncaster Works and cut up there when condemned in October 1955 from Bradford (Hammerton Street) shed. The station closed on 7 September 1964. *(M.E. Kirk/Martyn Reeve Collection)*

On 29 July 1954, an unidentified 2-8-0 Class '8F', running tender first, traverses the Awsworth viaduct, which was built between May 1873 and November 1875 and formed part of the Great Northern Railway Derbyshire Extension. The viaduct was built of red bricks used to create 43 arched spans with a total length of 1716 feet and a height of 60 feet. It was also known as Giltbrook viaduct (or Kimberley Viaduct, but known locally as Forty Bridges). It was demolished in 1973 to make way for the A610 bypass. *(M.E. Kirk/Martyn Reeve Collection)*

WD 'Austerity' 2-8-0 No. 90136 trundles through Basford North station on Christmas Eve 1953 with the 12.30pm Babbington Colliery-Bulwell Common mineral train. Built in 1943 by the North British Locomotive Company, Glasgow and condemned in April 1965 from Canklow shed, it was broken up at Cashmore's, Great Bridge. *(M.E. Kirk/Martyn Reeve Collection)*

An unkempt Gresley 2-6-0 Class 'K2' No. 61768 is working the 12.42pm Nottingham (Victoria)-Gedling and Carlton local train entering Basford North station on 24 December 1953. Manufactured in 1918 by the NBL Co. Glasgow, it was withdrawn from Colwick shed in January 1959 before being cut up at Darlington Works. The station closed on 7 September 1964. (M.E. Kirk/Martyn Reeve Collection)

Robinson 4-6-2T Class 'A5' No. 69817 is entering Basford North working the 1.12pm Pinxton-Nottingham (Victoria) local service on 24 December 1953. Built in 1917 at Gorton Works, this locomotive was condemned in April 1960 from Gorton shed and disposed of at Darlington Works. (M.E. Kirk/Martyn Reeve Collection)

Christmas Eve 1953 at Basford North. Gresley 2-6-0 Class 'K3' 61821 threads the junction with a westbound Goods train; built in 1924 at Darlington Works and withdrawn from Immingham shed in September 1962, it was cut up at Cashmore's, Great Bridge. With the cessation of passenger services on the GNR the station closed on 7 September 1964. *(M.E. Kirk/Martyn Reeve Collection)*

On 24 December 1953 Gresley 2-6-0 Class 'K2' 61738 heads the 12.57pm Colwick-Burton mineral train through the station at Basford North. It had been built in 1914 at Doncaster Works before its withdrawal in July 1959 from Colwick shed before being scrapped at Darlington Works. *(M.E. Kirk/Martyn Reeve Collection)*

The 9.20am (SO) Basford (North)-Scarborough has just left Basford North station on 3 July 1954 behind 4-6-0 Class 'B1' 61033 *Dibatag*. Built in 1947 at Doncaster Works and withdrawn from Canklow shed in March 1963 it was broken up where it had begun its life, at Doncaster Works. The rear portion of the train is composed of GCR 60' saloons. *(M.E. Kirk/Martyn Reeve Collection)*

Up mineral train hauled by Fowler 0-6-0 Class '4F' No. 44313 passing through Basford Vernon station on 23 December 1953. Built in 1927 at St Rollox Works, it was condemned from Nottingham shed in December 1959 and disposed of at T.W. Ward, Killamarsh. *(M.E. Kirk/Martyn Reeve Collection)*

Arriving at New Basford station on a misty 23 December 1953 is Thompson 4-6-0 'B1' No. 61209 working the 2.38pm Nottingham (Victoria) to Mansfield (Central) and Edwinstowe stopping train. Built in 1947 by the NBL Co. Glasgow and condemned from Colwick shed in September 1959, No. 61209 was disposed of by Albert Loom, Spondon. The station closed on 7 September 1964. *(M.E. Kirk/Martyn Reeve Collection)*

Composed of two Great Central clerestory coaches, the *Annesley Dido* forming the 11.45am Bulwell Common to Newstead (East) on 23 December 1953 is hauled by Hill 0-6-2T Class 'N7' No. 69691. Built in 1927 by Beardmore, Dalmuir, and withdrawn from Stratford shed in December 1960, it was scrapped at the nearby Works. Bulwell Common station closed on 4 March 1963. *(M.E. Kirk/Martyn Reeve Collection)*

On 2 May 1953 the 11.25am Worksop-Nottingham (Midland) is about to leave Bulwell Market station hauled by Whitelegg 4-4-2T Class '3P' No. 41943. Built in 1927 at Derby Works, it was disposed of there when withdrawn from Mansfield shed in February 1956. The station opened on 2 October 1848 as Bulwell; it was renamed Bulwell Market in August 1952 to distinguish it from other Bulwell stations. It was closed along with other stations along the line in 1964 and reopened in 1994 as part of the new Robin Hood line. (M.E. Kirk/Martyn Reeve Collection)

Leaving a smoke screen, Stanier 2-6-2T Class '3P' No. 40175 powers through Bulwell Market station on 23 December 1953 with the 11.37am Nottingham (Midland) to Mansfield (Town) and Worksop service. Built in 1938 at Derby Works and withdrawn from Kirkby-in-Ashfield shed in October 1961, it was disposed of by Albert Loom, Spondon. (M.E. Kirk/Martyn Reeve Collection)

The **8.44am Worksop** and Mansfield (Town) to Nottingham (Midland) service approaching Hucknall Byron station on 26 June 1954 headed by Fowler 2-6-4T Class '4P' No. 42339, built in 1929 at Derby Works, withdrawn from Bolton shed in September 1963 and broken up at Horwich Works. The station closed in 1964 and reopened in 1993 on the Robin Hood Line and was then simply called Hucknall. *(M.E. Kirk/Martyn Reeve Collection)*

Entering the Midland station at Hucknall Byron on 26 June 1954 is the 9.30am (SO) Nottingham-Worksop local stopping train hauled by Ivatt 2-6-0 Class '2MT' No. 46501, built in 1952 at Darlington Works and withdrawn in May 1967 from Newton Heath shed before being cut up at Drapers, Hull. *(M.E. Kirk/Martyn Reeve Collection)*

The 10.40am (SO) Edwinstowe-Nottingham (Victoria) local train entering Hucknall Central station on the Great Central line with Ivatt 0-6-2T Class 'N1' No. 69476 in charge on 26 June 1954. Built in 1912 at Doncaster Works, it was scrapped there when condemned from Colwick shed in March 1955. The station was closed on 4 March 1963 along with most other local stations on the line. *(M.E. Kirk/Martyn Reeve Collection)*

The 10.25am (SO) Mansfield (Town)-Nottingham (Midland) local service calls at Linby station on 26 June 1954, hauled by Fowler 0-6-0 Class '4F' No. 44415, built in 1927 at Derby Works, withdrawn in March 1960 from Mansfield shed and cut up at Crewe Works. Linby station was used predominately to serve the nearby colliery and closed in October 1964. Although the Robin Hood line reopened in 1993 Linby station did not. *(M.E. Kirk/Martyn Reeve Collection)*

Passing Linby Colliery (GNR Leen Valley line), on 26 June 1954 is Robinson 2-8-0 Class 'O4' No. 63839 with a Colwick bound freight train. Manufactured in 1918 at the North British Locomotive Company, Glasgow, it was withdrawn from Colwick shed in April 1959 and broken up at Gorton Works. *(M.E. Kirk/Martyn Reeve Collection)*

Perhaps it was an enlarged market day in Nottingham, judging by the number of passengers waiting at Sutton-in-Ashfield (Town) station to join the 1.25pm (SO) Shirebrook (North)-Nottingham (Victoria) stopping train. Gresley 2-6-0 Class 'K3' No. 61824 provided the motive power on 7 July 1956, having been built in 1924 at Doncaster Works, it was scrapped there when withdrawn from Woodford Halse shed in July 1961. *(M.E. Kirk/Martyn Reeve Collection)*

Arriving at Mansfield Central on 24 December 1953 is a Christmas extra, the 9.52am Nottingham (Victoria)-Skegness hauled by Thompson 4-6-0 Class 'B1' No. 61269, manufactured in 1947 by the North British Locomotive Co. Glasgow, withdrawn in December 1963 from Gorton shed and cut up at T.W.Ward, Killamarsh. *(M.E. Kirk/Martyn Reeve Collection)*

Pictured here at Mansfield Town station on 13 July 1954 is Whitelegg 4-4-2T Class '3P' No. 41943 working the 3.07pm Nottingham-Worksop stopping train. This locomotive was built in 1927 at Derby Works and broken up there when withdrawn in February 1956 from Mansfield shed. *(M.E. Kirk/Martyn Reeve Collection)*

Mansfield-allocated Whitelegg 4-4-2T 'Tilbury Tank' No. 41943 enters Mansfield Town station on 30 August 1955 heading the 3.40pm Worksop-Nottingham (Midland) stopping train. Built in 1927 at Derby Works, it was disposed of there when withdrawn from Mansfield shed with six months left in service. *(M.E. Kirk/Martyn Reeve Collection.*

A return Skegness to Doe Hill excursion train has reversed at Shirebrook West on 26 June 1954 and is now in the charge of a pair of Fowler 0-6-0s Class '4Fs' Nos. 44425 & 44082. The former, built in 1927 at Derby Works and withdrawn from Buxton shed in February 1965, was scrapped by Arnott Young, Parkgate. Manufactured by Kerr Stuart in 1925, No. 44082 was condemned from Canklow shed in September 1962 and cut up at Crewe Works. *(M.E. Kirk/Martyn Reeve Collection)*

Pictured at **Shirebrook** (West) station is a pair of Robinson 0-6-0s Class 'J11' No. 64379 and 64375(?) returning to Langwith Junction shed after hauling a Derbyshire Miners' Association excursion train from Skegness on 26 June 1954. Both locos were manufactured in 1904 by the North British Company, Glasgow; No. 64379 was withdrawn from Langwith Junction shed in September 1962 and disposed of at Gorton Works. *(M.E. Kirk/Martyn Reeve Collection)*

The 11.25am Worksop-Nottingham (Midland) local service is arriving at Sutton Junction on Christmas Eve 1953 headed by Stanier 2-6-2T Class '3P' No. 40168, built in 1937 at Derby Works, withdrawn from Kirkby-in-Ashfield shed in October 1961 and scrapped by A. Loom, Spondon. *(M.E. Kirk/Martyn Reeve Collection)*

A coal train from Shirebrook is passing the signal box at Edwinstowe on 26 June 1954 hauled by ex-WD 'Austerity' 2-8-0 No. 90018, manufactured in 1943 by the NBL Co. Glasgow, withdrawn from Doncaster shed in April 1966 and broken up at Drapers, Hull. *(M.E. Kirk/Martyn Reeve Collection)*

Empty stock in the platform at Edwinstowe to form the 4.20pm to Shirebrook North local on 26 June 1954 with Robinson 0-6-0 Class 'J11' No. 64337. Built by Beyer Peacock in 1903, it was withdrawn from Gorton shed in June 1961 and cut up at the adjacent Works. The train is composed of Great Central and North Eastern stock. The station lost its regular passenger service in 1955 but it continued to handle holiday traffic until 1964. *(M.E. Kirk/Martyn Reeve Collection)*

In a matter of five months the station will close. The 10.40am (SO) departure from Edwinstowe on 16 July 1955 to Mansfield and Nottingham is hauled by Robinson 4-6-2T Class 'A5' No. 69822, whilst sister engine No. 69828 will have charge of the 11.34am (SO) train to Nottingham via Shirebrook (North). Both locomotives were built in 1923 at Gorton Works and cut up at Darlington Works when condemned in November 1958 from Gorton and Colwick sheds respectively. *(M.E. Kirk/Martyn Reeve Collection)*

A short westbound Goods train, composed of six wagons and a brake van, is at Edwinstowe on 16 July 1955 hauled by Robinson 2-8-0 Class 'O4' No. 63635. Built in 1912 at Gorton Works and withdrawn from Langwith Junction shed in May 1962, this locomotive was scrapped at Doncaster Works. *(M.E. Kirk/Martyn Reeve Collection)*

The 10.52am Shirebrook (North) to Lincoln train leaving Edwinstowe on 16 July 1955 is seen here behind Robinson 4-6-2T Class 'A5' No. 69804. Built in 1911 at Gorton Works and condemned from Colwick shed in April 1958, it was broken up at Darlington Works. The station was opened by the Lancashire, Derbyshire and East Coast Railway in March 1897 and closed by British Railways on 2 January 1956, although the last train ran on 31 December 1955. *(M.E. Kirk/Martyn Reeve Collection)*

Eastern Region locomotives had gradually infiltrated the Midland area in the mid-1950s and this type superseded the 'D11' Directors that had been transferred to Sheffield (Darnall). Allocated to Lincoln (40A), five 'D16s' from Cambridge replaced the 'D11' engines in the spring of 1957, to be replaced by DMUs in 1958. This and the following photograph show 'D16' No. 62599 working a Lincoln-Nottingham local service in June 1957. *(M.E. Kirk/Martyn Reeve Collection)*

Certainly looking in better condition than some of the Holden 4-4-0 'D16s', No. 62599 is at Carlton & Netherfield on 2 June 1957 heading the 5.30pm Lincoln (St Marks)-Nottingham stopping train. Built in 1910 at Stratford Works, it was disposed of there after being withdrawn from Lincoln shed in September 1958. *(M.E. Kirk/Martyn Reeve Collection)*

Owing to Engineering Work on the London Road viaduct, the Derby-Grantham trains were diverted via Gedling with bus connections to and from Nottingham. Here, at Netherfield & Colwick on 8 April 1956, the 10.12am Derby (Friargate)-Grantham service is arriving hauled by Thompson 2-6-4T Class 'L1' No. 67749, which was built in 1948 by the NBL Co Glasgow, condemned from Colwick shed in December 1962 and broken up at Darlington Works. *(M.E. Kirk/Martyn Reeve Collection)*

A Yarmouth to Nottingham (Victoria) express leaving Netherfield & Colwick station is hauled by Gresley 2-6-0 Class 'K3' No. 61824 on 3 August 1957, which was built in 1924 at Darlington Works, withdrawn in July 1961 from Woodford Halse shed and broken up at Doncaster Works. *(M.E. Kirk/Martyn Reeve Collection)*

The 7.20am Nottingham (Midland-Newark (Castle) local stopping train headed by Fowler 2-6-4T Class '4P' No. 42373 at Colwick Vale on 26 March 1956. Built in 1929 at Derby works, it was withdrawn from Gorton shed in November 1960 and broken up at the nearby Works. *(M.E. Kirk/Martyn Reeve Collection)*

Near 'The Hall' signal box at Colwick Vale. A 1956 Easter Sunday excursion train, the 9.08am Basford (North) to Skegness is hauled by Gresley 2-6-0 Class 'K3' No. 61824, built in 1924 at Darlington Works, withdrawn from Woodford Halse shed in July 1961 and disposed of at Doncaster Works. (*M.E. Kirk/Martyn Reeve Collection*)

PLEASE RETAIN THIS BILL FOR REFERENCE   A89/R(H.D.)

EASTER HOLIDAYS - 1956

CHEAP TRIPS

TO

SKEGNESS

SUNDAY 1st APRIL 1956

61824

FROM	TIMES OF DEPARTURE		RETURN FARES Third Class	ARRIVAL TIMES ON RETURN	
	am	am	s d	pm	pm
BULWELL COMMON	...	9 48	11/6	9 58	...
HUCKNALL Central	...	9 55	11/6	9 50	...
KIRKBY-IN-ASHFIELD Central ...	...	10 9	11/6	9 36	...
SUTTON-IN-ASHFIELD Central	...	10 15	11/6	9 29	...
MANSFIELD Central	...	10 24	11/6	9 20	...
BASFORD North	9 8	...	11/6	...	10 48
NEW BASFORD	9 15	...	11/6	...	10 39
NOTTINGHAM Victoria	9 25	...	11/6	...	10 29
NETHERFIELD & COLWICK ...	9 34	...	11/3	...	10 19
	am	pm	Passengers return	pm	pm
SKEGNESS ... ... arrive	11 26	12 36	same day at ...	7 12	8 20

CHILDREN under three years of age, free ; three years and under fourteen, half-fares.

NOTICE AS TO CONDITIONS

These tickets are issued subject to the British Transport Commission's published Regulations and Conditions applicable to British Railways, exhibited at their stations or obtainable free of charge at Station Booking Offices.
For LUGGAGE ALLOWANCES also see these Regulations and Conditions.

RAIL TICKETS CAN BE OBTAINED IN ADVANCE AT STATIONS AND OFFICIAL RAILWAY AGENTS

Further information will be supplied on application to Stations, Official Railway Agents, or to W. B. CARTER, District Commercial Manager, DERBY. Telephone: Derby 42442, Extn. 204; or NOTTINGHAM Victoria, Telephone: Nottingham 44381, Extn. 32
A. G. CROXALL, District Commercial Manager, PETERBOROUGH. Telephone: Peterborough 4221, Extn. 31.

Travel in Rail Comfort

February 1956   BR 35000

BRITISH RAILWAYS

Arthur Gaunt & Sons (Printers) Ltd., Heanor, Derbyshire

Handbill associated with the previous photograph.
(M.E. Kirk/Martyn Reeve Collection)

The driver has now shut off steam on Gresley 2-6-0 Class 'K3' No. 61833 working the 9.45am Nottingham (Victoria)-Mablethorpe express, having passed the temporary permanent-way speed warning board at Colwick East Junction on Whit Sunday in 1956. It was built in 1924 at Darlington Works, withdrawn from Colwick shed in September 1961 and cut up at Doncaster Works. *(M.E. Kirk/Martyn Reeve Collection)*

Seen here photographed at Colwick shed on 10 June 1956 is Ivatt 0-6-0ST Class 'J52/1' No. 68785, built in 1896 by Neilson and withdrawn from Colwick shed in January 1958, later broken-up at Doncaster works. *(M.E. Kirk/Martyn Reeve Collection)*

Colwick Shed on 13 May 1956. Stirling 0-6-0ST Class 'J52' No. 68882, built in 1908 at Doncaster Works and disposed of there when withdrawn from Colwick shed in January 1958. Holden 0-6-0T Class 'J69' No. 68629, built in 1904 at Stratford Works and broken up at Gorton Works when condemned from Colwick shed in November 1959. Stirling 0-6-0ST Class 'J52/1' No. 68759, built in 1900 at Doncaster Works and cut up there when withdrawn in July 1956 from Colwick shed. *(M.E. Kirk/Martyn Reeve Collection)*

Raven 4-6-0 Class 'B16' No. 61477 awaits its next duty on Colwick shed on 13 May 1956. Built in 1920 at Darlington Works, it was cut up at its birthplace when withdrawn from York shed in February 1960. Colwick Motive Power Depot closed to steam 31 December 1966. *(M.E. Kirk/Martyn Reeve Collection)*

Another view of Colwick Shed in May 1956. Robinson 2-8-0 Class 'O4' No. 63657 was built in 1918 by Kitson and withdrawn from Colwick shed in September 1962 then cut up at Round Oak Steelworks. *(M.E. Kirk/Martyn Reeve Collection)*

Recently outshopped, Gresley 0-6-0T Class 'J50' No. 68927 is seen here at Colwick shed on 10 June 1956. Built in 1922 at Doncaster Works, it was scrapped there when withdrawn from Colwick shed in April 1961. *(M.E. Kirk/Martyn Reeve Collection)*

The 4.10pm from Southwell is ready to leave Rolleston Junction on 31 August 1955 with Johnson 0-4-4T Class '1P' No. 58085. Built in 1900 by Dubs & Co. Glasgow and condemned from Lincoln shed in April 1959, it was later cut up at Derby Works. The 2½ mile single track branch line from Rolleston (on the Midland Railway's Nottingham-Lincoln line) to Southwell was opened in 1847. The push-and-pull unit for passenger trains was finally withdrawn in June 1959, with goods traffic continuing for a further six years. *(M.E. Kirk/Martyn Reeve Collection)*

Robinson 4-4-0 Class 'D11' No. 62670 *Marne* is pictured at Lincoln (Central) station shunting empty stock on 7 March 1955. Built in 1922 at Gorton Works, it was condemned from Sheffield (Darnall) shed in November 1960 and disposed of at Doncaster Works. *(M.E. Kirk/Martyn Reeve Collection)*

Robinson 4-4-2T Class 'C13' No. 67427 is waiting to depart from Lincoln (Central) with the 1.15pm stopping train to Shirebrook (North) on 7 March 1955. Built in 1904 at Gorton Works, it was cut up there when withdrawn from Ardsley shed in January 1958. *(M.E. Kirk/Martyn Reeve Collection)*

Radcliffe-on-Trent station 12 July 1952. The 12.39pm departure to Nottingham Victoria with Hill 0-6-2T Class 'N7' No. 69615 is waiting to cross onto the Down line after the 10am Goods Waltham-on-Wolds to Colwick has passed hauled by a 0-6-0 'J6'. This locomotive was built in 1923 at Stratford Works and scrapped there when withdrawn from its neighbouring shed in September 1960. *(M.E. Kirk/Martyn Reeve Collection)*

In Darkest Notts, a description by M.E. Kirk, the 5.35pm Nottingham (Victoria)-Newark (North Gate) local service is arriving at Radcliffe-on-Trent on 18 July 1952 with Ivatt 0-6-0 Class 'J2' No. 65019 in charge. This locomotive was built in 1912 at Doncaster Works and scrapped there when withdrawn from Colwick shed in March 1953. *(M.E. Kirk/Martyn Reeve Collection)*

The 9.06am Colwick-Welham Sidings mineral train is passing through Barnstone on Saturday 12 July 1952 with WD 2-8-0 No. 90449 in charge. Built in 1944 at the Vulcan Foundry, it was withdrawn from Langwith Junction shed in January 1966 and disposed of at Drapers, Hull. Ready to depart from the other platform is the 8.20am Market Harborough-Nottingham (Victoria) stopping service with Johnson 4-4-0 Class '2P' No. 40534. This was built in 1899 at Derby Works, withdrawn in July 1959 from Nottingham shed and scrapped by T.W. Ward, Killamarsh. Barnstone station opened in 1879 and closed to regular traffic in 1953. *(M.E. Kirk/Martyn Reeve Collection)*

The 11.35am Nottingham (Victoria) to Grantham is arriving at Bingham station on 14 July 1954, hauled by Holden 4-6-0 Class 'B12' No. 61565, built in 1920 at Stratford Works and scrapped there when withdrawn in January 1957 from Peterborough (Spital Bridge) shed. *(M.E. Kirk/Martyn Reeve Collection)*

In the opposite direction, also at Bingham, on the same day, the 11.02am Grantham to Derby (Friargate) stopping train is worked by Ivatt/Gresley 0-6-0 Class 'J6' No. 64230, which was built in 1914 at Doncaster Works and disposed of there when withdrawn from Colwick shed in January 1958. *(M.E. Kirk/Martyn Reeve Collection)*

On 19 July 1952 Ivatt-Gresley 0-6-0 Class 'J6' No. 64197 arrives at Melton Mowbray (North) station working the 10.27am (SO) Leicester (Belgrave Road) to Grantham. Built in 1913 at Doncaster Works, it was also cut up there when condemned in October 1959 from Hitchin shed. Regular services ceased on 7 December 1953 but summer specials survived until 1962. *(M.E. Kirk/Martyn Reeve Collection)*

Fowler 0-6-0 Class '4F' No. 44403 is waiting to leave Melton Mowbray (Town) on 19 July 1952 with the 9.05am (SO) Kings Norton-Yarmouth (Beach) and Lowestoft (Central) train. Manufactured in 1927 by North British Locomotive Co. Glasgow, this locomotive was withdrawn from Coalville shed in June 1964 and broken up at Cashmore's, Great Bridge. *(M.E. Kirk/Martyn Reeve Collection)*

The 7.48am Peterborough (East)-Leicester (London Road) stopping train, is almost ready to leave Melton Mowbray (Mid) station on 27 July 1957, with long time (15C) resident 4-4-0 Class '2P' No. 40543, which was built in 1901 at Derby Works, withdrawn from Leicester shed in January 1961 and scrapped at Crewe Works. *(M.E. Kirk/Martyn Reeve Collection)*

Riddles BR Standard 4-6-0 Class '4MT' No. 75064 is about to leave the station in late July 1957, working the 12.15pm Leicester (London Road)-Kettering stopping train. Built in 1957 at Swindon Works and withdrawn from Aintree shed with less than ten years service, No. 75064 was disposed of at Cashmore's, Newport. The second coach is M10599M, derated from first to second. *(M.E. Kirk/Martyn Reeve Collection)*

On 26 July 1952, Ivatt 4-4-2T Class 'C12' No. 67386 is on station pilot duty at Kings Lynn. Built in 1903 at Doncaster Works, it was scrapped there when withdrawn in April 1958 from Kings Lynn shed. *(M.E. Kirk/Martyn Reeve Collection)*

Holden 0-6-0 'J19' 64655 is on the turntable at Kings Lynn Shed on 27 July 1952. This locomotive was built in 1916 at Stratford Works and scrapped there when withdrawn from Cambridge shed in August 1961. *(M.E. Kirk/Martyn Reeve Collection)*

In the South Wolds passing over the level crossing at Little Steeping in September 1954 is Thompson 'B1' 4-6-0 No. 61392, working a Holiday express, manufactured by the North British Locomotive Company, Glasgow in 1951, withdrawn in June 1965 from Colwick shed and cut up at T.W. Ward, Killamarsh. The station was closed to passenger traffic on 11 September 1961. *(Tony Smith)*

This photograph was taken from the Up platform at South Lynn on 30 August 1958, is of Fowler 0-6-0 Class '4F' No. 43937 with a Holiday express. It emerged from Armstrong Whitworth in 1921 and was withdrawn from Gorton shed in July 1963 before being disposed of at Horwich Works. South Lynn station was closed to passengers on 2 March 1959. *(Tony Smith)*

A view from the first coach of the 9.15am Nottingham (Victoria) to Skegness (Mablethorpe portion), entering Boston station on 30 June 1954, headed by, possibly, Gresley 'K3' No. 61896 which hauled the next day's return working. *(M.E. Kirk/Martyn Reeve Collection)*

A Down special express running through Boston station on 6 July 1957 headed by Gresley 4-6-0 Class 'B17' No. 61638 *Melton Hall*, which was built in 1933 at Darlington Works and withdrawn in March 1958 from March shed before being broken up at Doncaster Works. *(M.E. Kirk/Martyn Reeve Collection)*

Firsby station on 4 November 1952, the 9.05am Lincoln (Central)-Skegness train is leaving behind Thompson 4-6-0 Class 'B1'
No. 61258, tender first. The train has reversed and is now crossing the Up line to the Skegness branch, the junction of which can be
seen behind the starter signal. This loco was manufactured in 1947 by the North British Locomotive Co. Glasgow and withdrawn in
January 1964 from Lincoln shed; it was the last 'B1' broken up at Doncaster Works. *(M.E. Kirk/Martyn Reeve Collection)*

The 3.11pm Louth to
Willoughby local train
calls at Mablethorpe
on 1 July 1954 behind
Ivatt Class 'C12'
No. 67383, built in
1901 at Doncaster
Works and broken up
there when withdrawn
from Louth shed
in January 1955.
*(M.E. Kirk/Martyn
Reeve Collection)*

With passengers' luggage still to be loaded into the 11.50am (SO) Mablethorpe to Basford (North) express on 20 August 1955, this Gresley 2-6-0 'K2', No. 61729, is all fired up ready to go. Built in 1913 at Doncaster Works, it was withdrawn in June 1957 from Colwick shed and cut up at Gorton Works. The left hand train is the 11.06am (SO) Willoughby-Louth with Ivatt 'C12' No. 67364. *(M.E. Kirk/Martyn Reeve Collection)*

The 9.58am Louth to Firsby local train is approaching Seaholme road crossing in Mablethorpe on 19 August 1955 with Ivatt 4-4-2T Class 'C12' No. 67364. Built in 1899 at Doncaster Works, it was scrapped there when condemned in May 1956 from Louth shed. Leading coach is saloon E41344E. *(M.E. Kirk/Martyn Reeve Collection)*

The 2.29pm Sutton-on-Sea to Louth local train is pictured at Mablethorpe station on 22 August 1955, composed of GNR quadruplet (Gas-Lit) articulated set, comprised of (L to R) 47913, 47914, 47915, 47916, and hauled by 4-4-2T Class 'C12' No. 67379, which was built in 1901 at Doncaster Works and cut up there when withdrawn from New England shed June 1958. *(M.E. Kirk/Martyn Reeve Collection)*

Parker/Pollitt 0-6-2T Class 'N5' No. 69275 has arrived at Woodhall Junction station on 6 November 1952 with a local stopping train. It was built in 1900 by Beyer Peacock Ltd. and condemned from Lincoln shed in November 1955. The station closed on 5 October 1970. *(M.E. Kirk/Martyn Reeve Collection)*

In Three Counties (the title given to this image by M.E. Kirk) on 13 May 1953. On the LNWR Seaton-Uppingham branch from where passenger services were withdrawn in June 1960 and the line closed to all traffic in 1964. Here, the 11.10am Seaton to Uppingham train composed of Ivatt 4-4-2T Class 'C12' No. 67368 and push-pull trailer still in LMS livery waits to depart. Built in 1900 at Doncaster Works, this locomotive was scrapped there when withdrawn in October 1955 from Peterborough (Spital Bridge) shed. *(M.E. Kirk/Martyn Reeve Collection)*

Captioned by the photographer as *Rustic Rutland* on 13 May 1953, the Uppingham coach is running into the Bay after forming the 12.24pm from Uppingham with Ivatt 4-4-2T Class 'C12' No. 67368. After arriving at Seaton, the engine propels the coach onto the mainline, and then runs onto the other side of the platform. The coach brakes are released, running into the platform with the aid of a gradient. The Uppingham branch closed in 1960. *(M.E. Kirk/Martyn Reeve Collection)*

The 9.47am Seaton-Stamford local train is seen here on 13 May 1953 arriving at Morcott station with Ivatt 2-6-2T Class '2MT' No. 41278 providing the motive power. Built in 1950 at Crewe Works, it was broken up there when withdrawn from Llandudno Junction shed after just twelve years in service. Freight services finished on 4 May 1964 and passenger on 6 June 1966. *(M.E. Kirk/Martyn Reeve Collection)*

Johnson 4-4-0 Class '2P' No. 40326 formerly S&DJR No. 69, then LMS 326, is photographed at Market Harborough (LNWR) station on 13 May 1953 with an Engineers Inspection Saloon. It was built in 1921 at Derby Works and condemned from Derby shed in May 1956. The service on the original LNWR line was drastically reduced in 1960 and finally closed in 1966. *(M.E. Kirk/Martyn Reeve Collection)*

The 5¼ mile Wellingborough–Higham Ferrers branch closed to passenger traffic in June 1959 and to all traffic in 1969. Pictured here on 13 May 1953 at Wellingborough (Midland Road) station is the push-pull set hauled by Ivatt 2-6-2T Class '2MT' No. 41277. Built in 1950 at Crewe Works, it was withdrawn from a north-west shed in November 1962 and cut up at Horwich Works. (*M.E. Kirk/Martyn Reeve Collection*)

CHAPTER 10

INTERLUDE AT SAXBY STATION 27 JULY 1957

Formed of GER mainline corridor stock, the 12.55pm (Saturdays Only) Bourne-Saxby train has arrived on 19 July 1952 worked by Ivatt 2-6-0 Class '4' No. 43060, built in 1950 at Doncaster Works, withdrawn in December 1964 from Colwick shed and scrapped at Slag Reduction Co. Ltd., Ickles, Rotherham. *(M.E. Kirk/Martyn Reeve Collection)*

The 10.45am (SO) Kettering-Nottingham service calling at all intermediate stations, entering Saxby station on 27 July 1957 behind Johnson 4-4-0 Class '2P' No. 40493, which was built in 1897 at Derby Works and broken up by T.W.Ward, Killamarsh when withdrawn from Nottingham shed in July 1959. *(M.E. Kirk/Martyn Reeve Collection)*

Nottingham-allocated Fowler 0-6-0 Class '4F' No. 44401 provides the necessary motive power for an additional 8.35am (SO) Mansfield (Town) to Yarmouth express that included four all first-class coaches, seen here at Saxby station. Manufactured in 1927 by the North British Locomotive Company, Glasgow, it was withdrawn from Kirkby-in-Ashfield shed in June 1965 and scrapped by T.W. Ward, Killamarsh. *(M.E. Kirk/Martyn Reeve Collection)*

Having dispensed with its pilot engine 42421, Fowler 0-6-0 Class '4F' No. 44420 arrives at Saxby station with the 9.55am (SO) Derby to Cromer (Beach) & Yarmouth (Beach) express. Formed of twelve coaches, six for Yarmouth (Beach) and four for Cromer (Beach), the rear two coaches Lowestoft & Gorleston-on-Sea will be detached here and attached to the 10.52am service from Leicester (London Road). The M&GN line closed to passengers after the last train on 28 February 1959, although the section between Saxby and South Witham remained open for goods trains. Saxby station closed on 6 February 1961. *(M.E. Kirk/Martyn Reeve Collection)*

Entering the station behind Toton-allocated Fowler 0-6-0 Class '4F' No. 44376 is the 10.52am (SO) Leicester (London Road) to Lowestoft (Central) & Gorleston-on-Sea express. Here it will attach the portion detached off the 9.55am from Derby. Built in 1927 by Andrew Barclay, Sons & Co. Ltd. Kilmarnock, it was withdrawn from Kirkby-in-Ashfield shed in December 1964 and scrapped at Wards, Broughton Lane, Sheffield. *(M.E. Kirk/Martyn Reeve Collection)*

The 9.55am (SO) Derby to Cromer (Beach) and Yarmouth (Beach) via Bourne is departing from Saxby station behind Fowler 0-6-0 Class '4F' No. 44420 after detaching its rear portion. To the right of the picture, '4F' No. 44376 on the 10.52am (SO) Leicester to Lowestoft (Central) & Gorleston on Sea is waiting to set back onto the coaches in the platform detached off the 9.55am from Derby. The train will then run via Peterborough. *(M.E. Kirk/Martyn Reeve Collection)*

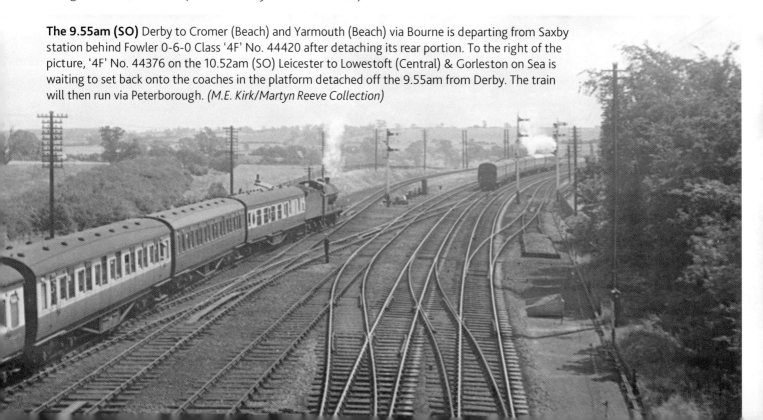

Pictured here dashing through Saxby station with twelve coaches in tow, is a 10.01am (SO) Nottingham to London (St Pancras), a relief to the 7.20am ex Bradford (Forster Square), may well have started from Leeds with Holbeck 'Jubilee' 4-6-0 Class '6P' 45658 *Keyes*, which was built in 1934 at Derby Works. This long-time Leeds (Holbeck) resident was withdrawn in May 1965 and cut up at Drapers, Hull. *(M.E. Kirk/Martyn Reeve Collection)*

One of several expresses each day booked to use the Midland route through Saxby station, rather than the line via Leicester and Market Harborough until the mid-1960s, 'Jubilee' 4-6-0 Class '6P' No. 45614 *Leeward Islands,* a Midland lines locomotive, except for a couple of months at Newton Heath shed in 1959, rushes through the station with the 7.20am Bradford (Forster Square) to London (St Pancras). Built in 1934 at Crewe Works, it was disposed of there when withdrawn from Derby shed in January 1964. *(M.E. Kirk/Martyn Reeve Collection)*

CHAPTER 11

GRANTHAM STATION

Holden designed 4-6-0 Class 'B12' No. 61574 arrives at Grantham station on 14 July 1954 with the 1.04pm service from Skegness. It was manufactured by Beyer Peacock Ltd in 1928 and withdrawn from Grantham shed in January 1957 before being broken up at Stratford Works. *(M.E. Kirk/Martyn Reeve Collection)*

The **12.03pm Bridlington-Kings** Cross express is entering the platform at Grantham in July 1954 hauled by 'A3' No. 60103 *Flying Scotsman*, built in 1923 at Doncaster Works as an 'A1' Pacific and emerging rebuilt in 1947 as an 'A3'. Withdrawn in January 1963 from Kings Cross shed, it was rescued for preservation by Mr A.F.Pegler and had various other owners before it was bought by the NRM for £2.3m in 2004. Work started on the restoration project in 2006 costing £4.2m and the locomotive was back on the main line in February 2016. *(M.E. Kirk/Martyn Reeve Collection)*

The driver has a look around Peppercorn 4-6-2 Class 'A1' No. 60135 *Madge Wildfire* at Grantham station on 14 July 1954 working an express for London (Kings Cross). Built in 1948 at Darlington Works, this was a victim of modernisation of the motive power fleet, rampant dieselisation resulting in a shamefully short working life of just a few days short of fourteen years in service before its withdrawal in November 1962 from Ardsley shed. It was cut up at Doncaster Works. *(M.E. Kirk/Martyn Reeve Collection)*

Approaching the station at Grantham in July 1954 is the 1.18pm Kings Cross-Bradford (Exchange) with Peppercorn 4-6-2 Class 'A1' No. 60130 *Kestrel* doing the honours. Built in 1948 at Darlington Works, it was withdrawn from Ardsley shed in October 1965 and scrapped at Doncaster Works. *(M.E. Kirk/Martyn Reeve Collection)*

Changing engines on long distance trains at intermediate stations became quite common in the 1950s to balance crew workings. Here at Grantham on 14 July 1954, Gresley 2-6-2 Class 'V2' No. 60865 is coming off the 11.25am Leeds (Central)-Kings Cross express to be replaced by Peppercorn 'A1' No. 60156 *Great Central*. Built in 1939 at Darlington Works, No. 60865 was withdrawn in June 1965 from Gateshead shed and disposed of by Ellis Metals, Swalwell. *(M.E. Kirk/Martyn Reeve Collection)*

Having replaced the Gresley 'V2' No. 60865 on the 11.25am from Leeds (Central), Peppercorn Pacific 'A1' No. 60156 *Great Central* is ready to leave on the final leg of the journey to Kings Cross. No. 60156 was built in 1949 at Doncaster Works and withdrawn from York shed in May 1965 and cut up at Clayton & Davie, Dunston-on-Tyne. *(M.E. Kirk/Martyn Reeve Collection)*

On 14 July 1954, the 11.45am Newcastle-Kings Cross was worked as far as Grantham by Gresley 'A3' Pacific No. 60061 *Pretty Polly*. Taking over 'The Northumbrian' is Peppercorn 4-6-2 Class 'A1' No. 60128 *Bongrace* now complete with headboard. Built in 1949 at Doncaster Works, the 'A1' was withdrawn from Doncaster shed in January 1965 and broken up at Drapers, Hull. *(M.E. Kirk/Martyn Reeve Collection)*

A pair of Ivatt 4-4-2Ts at Grantham on 15 July 1955. Class 'C12' No. 67362 is on station pilot duty with sister engine No. 67391 on shed. Built in 1900 & 1907 respectively, at Doncaster Works, they were both scrapped there when condemned from Grantham shed in January 1958. *(M.E. Kirk/Martyn Reeve Collection)*

The 8.55am (MWFO) Tyne Commission Quay-Kings Cross express at Grantham on 15 July 1955 is headed by Gresley 'A3' No. 60072 *Sunstar*. Manufactured in 1924 by the North British Locomotive Company, Glasgow, it was condemned in October 1962 from Heaton shed and cut up at Doncaster Works. *(M.E. Kirk/Martyn Reeve Collection)*

On an unidentified Up Kings Cross working on 8 October 1955 is Gresley 'A3' Pacific No. 60077 *The White Knight*. Built by the NBL Co. Glasgow and withdrawn in July 1964, it was scrapped by Arnott Young, Carmyle. This locomotive had an all too brief allocation to Leeds (Holbeck) shed in 1960, working over the Settle & Carlisle route until displaced by BR Sulzer 'Type 4' diesels. *(M.E. Kirk/Martyn Reeve Collection)*

Peppercorn 'A1' Pacific No. 60134 *Foxhunter* is seen here working a relief to the 10.35am Leeds (Central)-Kings Cross at Grantham on 2 June 1957. Built in 1948 at Darlington Works, it was withdrawn from Leeds (Neville Hill) shed in October 1965 and disposed of at T.W.Ward Beighton. *(M.E. Kirk/Martyn Reeve Collection)*

Running close behind *Foxhunter* at Grantham on 2 June 1957 is Gresley 'A4' Pacific No. 60013 *Dominion of New Zealand* (headboard reversed) working the 10.35am Leeds (Central) to Kings Cross express. Built in 1937 at Doncaster Works, it was broken up there when withdrawn in April 1963 from Kings Cross shed. *(M.E. Kirk/Martyn Reeve Collection)*

Replenishing its water tank at Grantham on 2 June 1957 is Gresley 4-6-2 Class 'A3' No. 60054 *Prince of Wales*, working a relief to the 10.10am Kings Cross-Leeds (Central). Built in 1924 at Doncaster Works (named *Manna* until November 1926), it was withdrawn from New England shed in June 1964 and cut up at A. King & Sons, Norwich. *(M.E. Kirk/Martyn Reeve Collection)*

On 6 July 1957, Gresley 2-6-2 Class 'V2' 60932 is working the 8.55am Tyne Commission Quay-Kings Cross, ready to depart from Grantham station. Built in 1941 at Doncaster works and withdrawn in May 1964 from York shed, it was disposed of at Swindon Works. *(M.E. Kirk/Martyn Reeve Collection)*

A schoolboy looks on admiringly as an Up relief express from the north to London (Kings Cross) runs into Grantham station at 3.37pm on 28 July 1962 with Gresley 'A4' Pacific No. 60033 *Seagull* in charge. This locomotive was built in 1938 at Doncaster Works and broken up there when withdrawn from Kings Cross shed in December 1962. *(M.E. Kirk/Martyn Reeve Collection)*

On 19 August 1961, an admirer at Grantham station studies Gresley 'A4' Pacific No. 60022 *Mallard,* which, as 4468, holds the world record as the fastest steam locomotive. Built in 1938 at Doncaster Works and withdrawn from Kings Cross Shed in April 1963, it is preserved at the National Rail Museum, York. *(M.E. Kirk/Martyn Reeve Collection)*

The doyen of the Gresley 'A4' Pacifics, No. 60022 *Mallard* is seen here at the head of a Kings Cross bound express at Grantham on 28 July 1962. *(M.E. Kirk/Martyn Reeve Collection)*

On 11 June 1962 Gresley 'A4' Pacific No. 60006 *Sir Ralph Wedgwood* (formerly *Herring Gull*, name changed in January 1944 to replace 4469 destroyed at York) prepares to leave Grantham station with the 8.35am Tyne Commission Quay to Kings Cross express. Built in 1938 at Doncaster Works, it was withdrawn in September 1965 from Aberdeen (Ferryhill) shed - where its last duties were on the 3-hr services to Glasgow - and scrapped at Motherwell Machinery & Scrap, Wishaw. (*M.E. Kirk/Martyn Reeve Collection*)

APPENDIX

LONDON MIDLAND OPERATING AREAS

DERBY DISTRICT

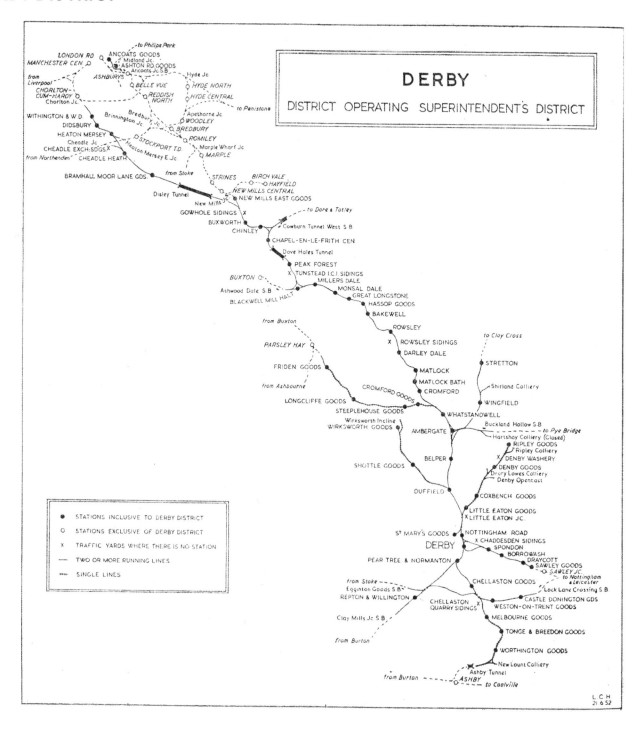

NOTTINGHAM DISTRICT

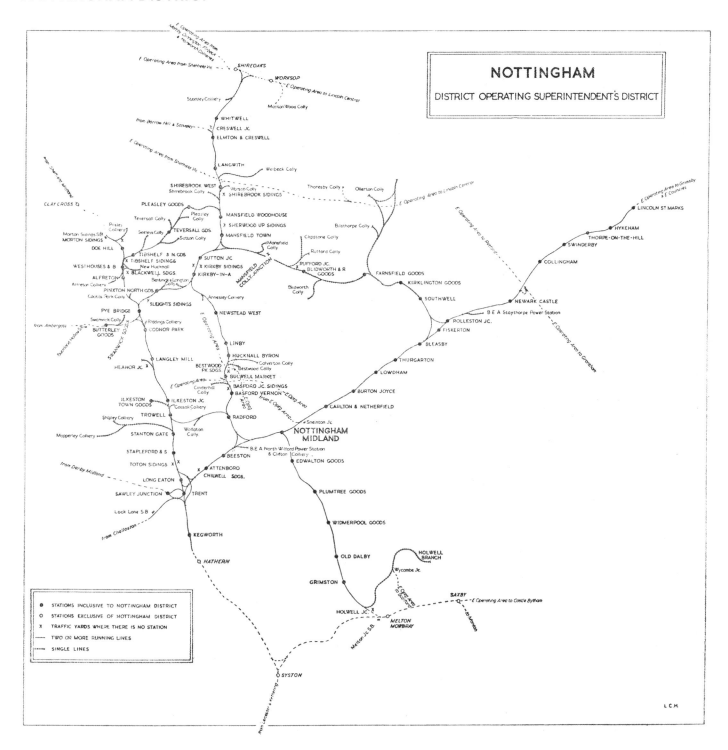

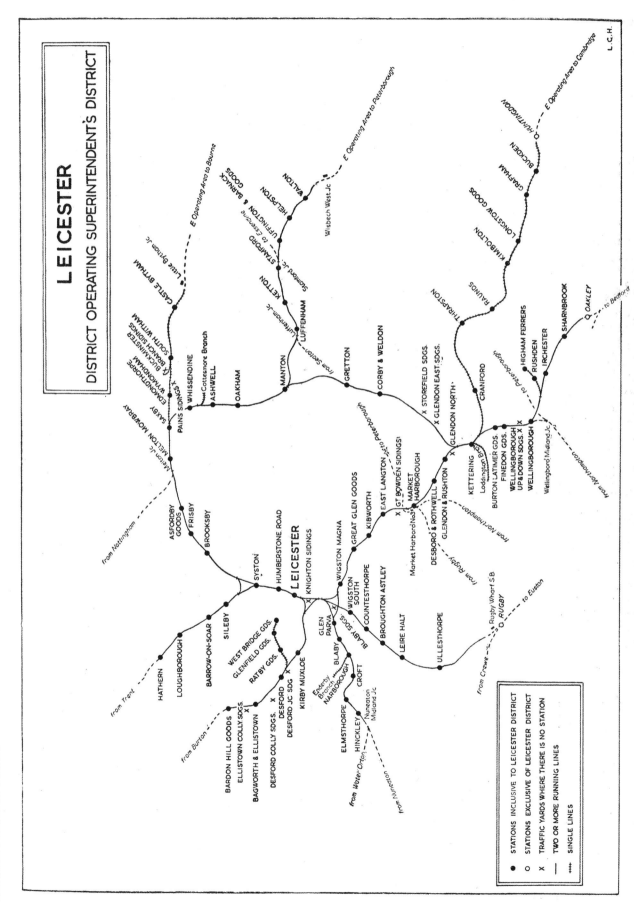

LEICESTER
DISTRICT OPERATING SUPERINTENDENT'S DISTRICT

L.C.H.

STATIONS INCLUSIVE TO LEICESTER DISTRICT
STATIONS EXCLUSIVE OF LEICESTER DISTRICT
TRAFFIC YARDS WHERE THERE IS NO STATION
TWO OR MORE RUNNING LINES
SINGLE LINES

LEICESTER CONTROL G.C. RUNNING SHEETS 1961

SHEET 1.

NO. 1 SECTION   DOWN PASSENGER SHEETS   SUMMER 1961

No.	Train	Days Run	WFD	RY	LUTT.	LESTER	L'BORO.	REMARKS
1587	10/15(FO) ME-GW	SO	12.2	12.20	12.29	12.42 / 12.43	12.54	Until 2nd Sept.
1N34	9/40 Swindon-York (SX)	MX	12.15	12.40	12.49	1.2 / 1.12	1.25 / 1.28	
1S??	11/0(FO) ME-GW	SO	12.43	1.1	1.9	1.22 / 1.24	1.37	From 15 July to 19 Aug.
1N35	9/25 Dover-Newc. Th.O	FO	1.44	2.2	2.10	2.23 / 2.29	2.41	16 June – 14 July
1N5	10/22 Dover-Newc. T.O.	WO	2.45	3.3	3.11	3.24 / 3.30	3.42	26 July – 30 Aug.
1N5	10/22 Dover-Newc. Th.O	FO	2.45	3.3	3.11	3.24 / 3.30	3.42	Comm. 21 July.
1M35	1.35 ME — NM	MX	3.13	3.43	3.52	4.5 / 4.12	4.23	
1E0?	5.20 LR — LDNO	SO				5.20	5.32 / 5.34	July 1st – 2nd Sept.
2D5?	5.40 WFD — NM	D	5.40	6.5	6.15 / 6.16	6.41 / 6.55	7.16 / 7.21	
1E4?	6.45 LR — Sheff	D				6.45	7.1 / 7.2	
1E54	7.20 LR — Cloo	SO				7.20	7.34 / 7.36	29 July – 12 Aug.
1E42	7.30 LR — Sheff	D				7.30	7.46 / 7.47	
1N42	7.50 LR — Scarb	SO				7.50	8.4 / 8.6	17 24 June. 1st July 26 Aug. 2 Sep

NO. 5 SECTION   DOWN PASSENGER SHEETS   SUMMER 1961   SHEET 2.

No.	Train		Days Run	WFD	RY	LUTT.	LESTER	L'BORO	REMARKS
2B5?	3.40 ME	NM	D	6.35	7.8	7.18/7.19	7.44/8.0	8.21/8.23	—
2B8?	7.35 RY	LE	D		7.35	7.45/7.47	8.12		
3X?6	6.50 BAN	York	MSX	7.55	7.50	8.1½	8.18/8.38	8.52	
I43	8.20 LR	Scarb.	SO				8.20	8.34/8.36	8 July – 19 Aug.
3?6	6.50 BAN	York	SO	7.22	7.50	8.1	8.24/8.42	8.56	
I86	8.55 LR	Skeg	SO				8.55	9.9/9.11	
IE9C	9.15 LR	Mable	SO				9.15	9.29/9.31	
2D5?	9.30 LR	NM	D				9.30	9.51/9.52	
2H9	9.55 RY	NM	D		9.55	10.5/10.6	10.31/10.35	10.56/10.58	
ID5?	8.40 ME	NM	D	10.26	10.51	11.1/11.2	11.17/11.19	11.31/11.33	
IN72	8.5 B'mouth	Newc.	SO	11.49	12/12	12/21	12/34/12/39	12/53/12/55	8 July – 19 Aug.
2B66	1/0 LR	Cfield	D		1/9	1/19/1/20	1/0	1/21/1/22	
2F52	12/45 WFD	LR	W.SO	12/45			1/45		

NO. 5 SECTION   DOWN PASSENGER SHEETS   SUMMER 1961   SHEET 3.

No.	Train	Days Run	WFD	RY	LUTT	LESTER	L'BORO	REMARKS
1N81	8.15 S'Sea – Newc	FO	1/10	1/37	1/46	1/59 / 2/4	2/18 / 2/20	7 July – Aug. 25th
1N81	8110 S'Sea – York	SO	1/10	1/37	1/46	1/59 / 2/4	2/18 / 2/20	8th July – Aug. 26th
1F58	2/10 RY LR	D		2/10	2/20 / 2/21	2/?6		
1D35	12/25(SO) ME NM / 12/40 SX	D	2/20	2/41	2/51 / 2/52	3/7 / 3/11	3/23 / 3/25	
1F63	10.25 Poole – BD	SO	3/4	3/28	3/37	3/50 / 3/56	4/10 / 4/12	
1E46	10.14 Hast SD	SO	3/16	3/39	3/48	4/1 / 4/6	4/20 / 4/22	15 July – 25th August
1E52	1k.0 Bmouth SD	SO	3/23	3/48	3/57	4/10 / 4/16	4/30 / 4/32	
1N83	11.16 Bmouth Newc	SX	3/33	3/55	4/4	4/16 / 4/22	4/34 / 4/35	
1N83	11.16 Bmouth–Newc.	SO	3/34	3/58	4/7	4/20 / 4/29	4/43 / 4/46	
2D53	5/15 LR NM	D				5/15	5/36 / 5/39	
1H33	12/27 Margate–LR	SO	4/34	4/58	5/9 / 5/11	5/26		22 July – 12 Aug.
1D36	5/45 LR NM	SX				5/45	5/59 / 6/c	
1E31	12/13 RAMS – DY	SO	4/55	5/19	5/30 / 5/32	5/47 / 5/51	6/5 / 6/7	Until Sept 2nd.

NO.5 SECTION   DOWN PASSENGER SHEETS   SUMMER 1961   SHEET 4.

No.	Train		Days Run	WFD	RY	LUTT.	LESTER	L'BORO.	REMARKS
1M29	12/32 Hast	MR	SO	5/0	5/24	5/38	5/55 6/1	6/13	July 1st – Sept. 2nd
2D57	5/5 WFD	NM	D	5/5	5/33	5/43 5/44	6/9 6/15	6/36 6/38	
1D37	4/25 ME	NM	D	6/14	6/35	6/45 6/46	7/1 7/5	7/17 7/19	
1M46	3/2 Pompey	NM	SO	6/27	6/51	7/0	7/13 7/18	7/32 7/34	15th July – 26th Aug.
2D53	7/25 LR	NM	SO				7/25	7/46 7/49	
3F58	7/25 RY	LR (E.Coa)	SO		7/25	7/35	7/55		
2E66	5/0 ME	Cfied	D	7/22	7/47	7/57 7/58	8/23 8/27	8/48 8/50	
2F58	8/15 RY	LR	D		8/15	8/25 8/26	8/51		
1E55	4/57Pompey	Sheff.	SO	8/23	8/46	8/55	9/8 9/13	9/27 9/29	Comm. 24 June
1S84	7/25 ME	Perty	SO	9/6	9/26	9/35	9/52 9/57	10/11	
1S84	7/25 ME	Prth	M WO	9/23	9/41	9/49	10/6 10/8	10/20	
1S84	7/25 ME	Glas	T Th.O	9/23	9/41	9/49	10/6 10/8	10/20	
2D53	10/15 Lr.	NM	D				10/15	10/36 10/37	

NO. 5 SECTION   DOWN PASSENGER SHEETS   SUMMER 1961   SHEET 5.

No.	Train	Days Run	WFD	RY	LUTT	LESTER	L'BORO.	REMARKS
1E50	7/30 Swindon–Sheff.	FSX	9/43	10/9	10/18	10/31 / 10/44	10/53	
1E50	7/30 Swindon–Sheff.	FSO	9/43	10/9	10/20 / 10/22	10/37 / 10/46	11/0 / 11/2	
1?20	8/45 ME–PN & L'pool.	S.X	10/38	10/58	11/7	11/24 / 11/33	11/47	
NO6	8/50 ME York	SX	10/52	11/12	11/21	11/38 / 11/44	11/58	
135	9/35 ME EO	FO	11/20	11/38	11/46	11/59 / 12.0	12.12	21st July–18th Aug.
135	9/35 ME EO	SO	11/20	11/38	11/46	11/59 / 12.0	12.12	
1S86	9/45 ME EO	FO	11/30	11/48	11/56	12.9 / 12.10	12.22	Until 1st Sept.
1S86	9/50 ME EO	SO	11/30	11/48	11/56	12.9 / 12.10	12.22	
1M10	9/55 ME	MR & LL SX	11/48	12.14	12.23	12.36 / 12.48	1.2 / 1.5	8th, 15, 22, 29 July 5 & 12 Aug. only.

Abbreviations

EO	EDINBURGH	Ban	BANBURY
GW	GLASGOW	Bmouth	BOURNEMOUTH
LL	LIVERPOOL	Clee	CLEETHORPES
LR	LEICESTER	Hast	HASTINGS
ME	MARYLEBONE	LDNO	LLANDUDNO
MR	MANCHESTER	Mable	MABLETHORPE
NM	NOTTINGHAM	Newc	NEWCASTLE
PN	PRESTON	Rams	RAMSGATE
RY	RUGBY	Scarb	SCARBOROUGH
WFD	WOODFORD	S'Sea	SOUTHSEA
		Skeg	SKEGNESS

General Map of Rail Connections with Lincoln

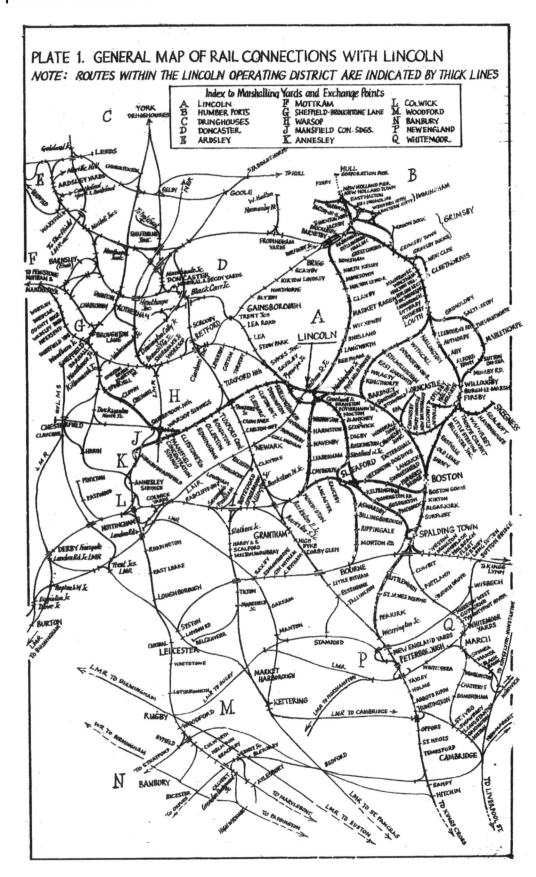

INDEX

LOCOMOTIVE CLASSES/TYPES

London Midland & Scottish

London & North Eastern

British Railways Standard Locomotives

LOCOMOTIVE MANUFACTURES

MOTIVE POWER DEPOTS

SCRAPYARDS

PERSONNEL/VARIOUS

STATIONS/LOCATIONS